The Six Sales Powers to
UNSTOPPABLE SELLING

The Six Sales Powers to UNSTOPPABLE SELLING

Duane Marino

Prominent Books

ISBN 10: 1942389043

ISBN 13: 978-1-942389-04-0

Published by Prominent Books, LLC

Prominent Books and the Prominent Books logo are property of Prominent Books, LLC.

TABLE OF CONTENTS

INTRODUCTION
The Greatest Profession in the World 1

CHAPTER 1
The Five P's of Sales Success 9

CHAPTER 2
Committing to Long-Term Success 25

CHAPTER 3
Performance Psychology 39

CHAPTER 4
Shortcuts to Success 51

CHAPTER 5
Understanding Our Industry:
Statistics vs. Trends 69

CHAPTER 6
Seven Industry Trends... 75

CHAPTER 7
The Six Sales Powers 99

CHAPTER 8
Your Power of Customer Service 109

CHAPTER 9
Your Power of Communication 141

CHAPTER 10
Your Power of Relationships 179

CHAPTER 11
Your Power of Effective Use of Time...................209

CHAPTER 12
Your Power of Understanding Body Language ..221

CHAPTER 13
Your Power of Focus 233

CHAPTER 14
Introspection 251

BONUS CHAPTER 15
Appointment Lock Down.....................................265

AFTERWORD 269

INDEX 275

DEDICATION

This book is dedicated to my best friend, hero and biggest fan, my late father, Ottavio Marino, the world's number-one dad in the history of all dads—one of the most intelligent, quirky and passionate people I have been blessed to know and learn from. I wonder almost daily how and why I was so lucky to have him as my father. My huge desires to learn, grow and succeed were fueled by him. When confronted with a life problem, I often reflect on "WWDD" (What Would Dad Do?)

The answers that come to me are always the right ones. I reach further because I stand on his shoulders and the shoulders of many other great people I have met, studied, modeled and worked with over the years.

Reader, if you want to learn how to improve your sales and life, you have come to the right spot. As they say, when the student is ready, the teacher will appear. So the real question is, are you ready?

"We spend every day of our lives trying to sell what we believe in, so we might as well learn how to perfect it."

—Duane Marino

Introduction

The Greatest Profession
In the World

Everybody is in sales in some way. Whether a child convincing her father to buy her an ice cream or a professional closing someone to buy a product or service, we sell every day of our lives.

In its rawest sense, sales is simply the activity of convincing another to do something. With ethics and a moral code intact, selling is the most important activity of social intercourse to ever exist. Many would argue, including myself, that sales is the greatest profession in the world.

In a world of much unfairness, where, at best, a winner and a loser result from our social activities, sales allows for the rare occurrence of both sides winning. Seldom are such fair and amicable circumstances even possible. But through proper selling techniques and practices, there is no loser.

What's incredible is, I have found that the more capable we are of selling, the more successful we will be in business and life in general. Just the same, the more successful we are at it, the more we're able to significantly influence the lives of others. Not only is it possible to become very rich as a great salesperson, at the risk of sounding a bit dramatic, it is nevertheless true that you can also live a rewarding life by making the world a better place to live in and by helping others to get what they want.

With all of its value and importance, there is yet an unshakable stigma, historically speaking, that haunts this field—perhaps because of the snake oil salesmen who proceeded us—and thus, the bad rap we get as being "the bad guy". Still, the shortsightedness of others doesn't phase us. With callused skin, we stick to the plan of helping as many people as possible to live and/or survive better through what we help them to possess. The very successful salespeople proceed with confidence, knowing just how vitally important they are in the overall scheme of things.

There are still a few "salespeople" around who are keeping the swindler tradition alive. Making sure that we ourselves follow a sales code of conduct will help to bring about their eventual extinction; hopefully leaving only good things to say about this profession. The easiest way is by seeking to offer more than what was expected by our customers. The pseudo-salesperson never makes it in the long-run through their own undoing. We will discuss the best practices for long-term success in this book.

The best salespeople get the vast majority of their income from self-perpetuated, positive word-of-mouth promotion and all of the repeat and referral business that comes from it. We refer to this level of selling as being "Angelic".

"Angels", as I call them, are considered true sales professionals. They produce so many happy, loyal customers that they never have to rely on new traffic. The Arch Angel in this regard is a friend and one of my mentors, Joe Girard. Joe is famously known as the "World's Greatest Salesman" as awarded by *The Guinness Book of World Records*.

This book shares the essentials to becoming very successful in your field. Mastering sales will turn whatever profession you are currently in into a more fun and lucrative career.

No matter what you do for a living, in order to advance, you need to sell yourself. Life is easier when you learn how to sell yourself to your friends, neighbors, coworkers, customers and your children. Selling a product is a one-time proposition. Selling yourself is a lifetime scenario of loyalty in repeat sales among other very favorable things.

The great profession of selling is, without a doubt, the most pervasive, permanent, persistent and lucrative of all professions ever created. We make it possible for enterprises to run and entire societies to operate. Salespeople are the suppliers of monetary fuel—the *only* type of fuel that any and all entities of productivity can live by.

We do what most people could never do even if their lives depended on it. The level of braveness we possess is seldom seen or needed in most other positions. Relentlessly, we face off with others who often bring their worst sides to the table, clawing with deep-seated irrationalities so commonly connected with money. We help them through their struggle so they can get what they really need. For whatever reason, the car business in particular brings out the dark side of many consumers.

We push through to keep the fuel coming in so that more things of value can be produced and provided to those who need them. We keep the lights on and phones connected for yet another week. We are the lifeline to every conceivable establishment. We make it possible for activities to keep going month after month; year in, year out.

With so much at stake and a lot to contend with, without a doubt, we need all the help we can get. It's important to continue to learn new things and strive to improve our approaches and techniques to make them more effective.

Sales is, if we want to be the best, an ongoing adventure of increasing ability. I believe this book will move anyone who is interested in expanding their horizons light years ahead of their industry.

Even with all of the importance and necessity there is with regard to selling, to the best of my knowledge, you can't get a university degree in *how* to actually sell. Still, it is very important for yourself and others to sell like an angel. To sell like one, you are going to need to get a *street issue* Ph.D. in Sales and Sales Psychology, and this "degree" needs to include the *six powers* to unstoppable selling.

The reason these six powers are vital is that they're the underlying support upon which your exceptional success in selling relies and can escalate. For me, success is all about seeing results as quickly and simply as possible. Success and failure leave clues, and because of this, success can be not only understood, but also replicated.

I have a passion for teaching others what I've been so blessed to notice and taught over the past few decades. I've been in the automotive profession since the early 80s and the training profession since the early 90s, and I'd achieved some great insight about how Angels think when Joe Girard called me out of the blue one day.

I will never forget the day my cell phone rang in 2007 while I was at one of my homes—my condo in Toronto. After saying hello, I heard, "Mr. Marino, this is Joe Girard." I nearly fell over. My reaction had him jokingly ask me, "What's the matter, kid? You never heard of me?" I said that I most certainly had. I quickly sat down on my couch and proceeded to do a lot of listening.

That was the beginning of a great mentorship and friendship that continues to shape me to this day. It was also the beginning of a new life for me simply because of what I have learned about selling like an angel. Just as companies need money to flourish, so too do we as individuals need it in order to live life stress-free. With a strong, sufficient income, we can have the power to do what we want and create big results. In this book, I share the most important aspects of what allowed me to become successful as a true professional salesperson and sales coach.

I never thought I would actually meet Joe, as my inspiration and the practices behind how to become a top sales professional was, to a degree, originally shaped by his books and, oddly enough, a can of tomatoes (more about this in a moment).

One of the most important skills you can learn in life and sales is to determine the small differences that make significant results for you. In other words, it's important to realize exactly which activities bring forth the biggest results. The easiest and most effective way to do this is to first observe what a highly-effective person is doing, and then in a sort of reverse-engineering manner, start to eliminate their behaviors, beliefs and actions, piece by piece, until you no longer get the desired result. *That which cannot be eliminated without affecting the result is then determined to be crucial* and therefore must be assimilated by anyone wanting a similar outstanding result! A great example of this is an experience I had with none other than a can of tomatoes.

One day, while making tomato sauce, I wondered, if I were to remove the onions from my recipe, whether I'd still have tomato sauce. My conclusion was that I would. Of course, it wouldn't taste the same, but it would still be a tomato sauce. Would the same be for the garlic? Yes. The olive oil? Yup. The salt, pepper, basil, parsley or hot peppers? For sure. Then I wondered, *What about the tomatoes?* This was the point where my sauce would no longer be a tomato sauce.

A light then went off in my head that led me to ask myself, *What are a top salesperson's tomatoes?!* In other words, what are the crucial, non-removable traits of outstanding salespeople? What key skills must they possess? And, if these skills were removed completely, what is it that would make them totally unable to sell?

I was onto something big. I knew that if I could just figure that out, I would know the most important traits of the greatest salespeople; and with that recipe in hand, help create massive success!

Over the next few months, I determined that there were six crucial skills or "Six Sales Powers" that a salesperson must possess or their selling would be crippled and their success limited.

One of the most important skills you can learn in life and sales is to determine the small differences that make significant results for you.

Then, I held those six traits up to every outstanding sales person I could think of and, to my surprise, discovered that their sales successes came from their mastery of these six areas! In fact, in my opinion, *all* outstanding salespeople or "Angels" have mastered these six areas or traits to the most extreme levels.

Also, as I use various examples of real-life strategies from myself and other great and notable sales professionals, I ask that you look for the "message in the bottle" or the meaning behind the message. Rather than trying to use all the examples exactly, directly or literally, see the points that are being made, and modify the techniques so you can adapt them to match your personality. This way, you can market along the same lines and still get the desired effect.

This book is about the principles, practices and psychology of sales as taught to me by outstanding salespeople, years of formal study, countless hours of observation, and almost three decades of real-world experience. Although the teachings are slanted towards car sales, the information provided applies to any type of selling no matter what field you might be in.

At the time of this writing, I have trained and coached tens of thousands of salespeople and managers, and personally consulted for over 400 dealerships in Canada and the USA. I have been able to observe and get to know the best, the worst and everything in between.

I share in this book my insight and essential key factors to sales success—the six powers to unstoppable selling, among other things, such as the Five P's of Sales Success, that support these powers. With these six under your belt and the specifics of selling in the real world, you will gain a much deeper insight into how to bring the level of success you have now to a whole new level.

For greater understanding, you will find "Duane Brain Tips", which are additional information that relates to the immediate text, and enlightening quotes throughout the book. Be sure to take note of them as well.

CHAPTER 1

The Five P's of Sales Success

There are ways to do things in business—in sales specifically. Some are more effective than others. When you can find certain activities that are vital and return the most for your investment of time and energy, they become the things that should be embraced and used in your daily routine.

I begin many of my workshops with a discussion of the Five P's because they govern how to conduct any type of business. They are as follows:

- Principles
- Practices
- Psychology
- Patterns
- Probability

Each of these are covered below:

PRINCIPLES

It's important to never forget that there are principles (or laws) that exist in sales. They can be referred to as laws or principles because they can be witnessed as happening all the time with little to no exception. It doesn't matter whether you're in Halifax or Honolulu (and I've worked in both); they are relevant.

The consistency of a law or principle can be shown with the following example: if you throw a pen up in the air, you can be certain that it is going to fall back to earth. We've come to know this fact by either experiencing it ourselves or through studying the law of gravity.

Laws and principles, already on the books, are simply documented experiences of empirical fact from what others who have come before us have realized and decided to share. Sales pains, suffering and frustration can be avoided simply by studying some known and undeniable knowledge of the masters. And if we can study and come to know things that are widely and consistently true almost all the time, it is a very powerful thing in allowing us to reach our goals.

Taking the gravity example further, if I were to throw a pen up in the air and walk underneath its descending path with the hopes of not being hit by it, the law of gravity puts the odds against me. And if I were to complain about getting hit in the head by the pen, I would be considered a fool or stupid for ignoring the law of gravity. But foolishness and stupidity in sales are, in most cases, the outcome of not understanding or obeying the important principles or laws of sales.

You will find that the best sales people spend the most time in their offices, and the best managers spend the most time on the sales floor! You will never get any great leads, strong skills, wonderful habits or a good attitude from hanging out in the huddle! This is a law.

PRACTICES

The second P is "Practices". Practices are strategies, techniques and behavioral patterns … things we can do to put us in front of more prospects and then get them to actually buy, such as the word tracks and sound bytes I mention later in this book. They are the way we speak, the way we listen, our product presentations, our timing and other important things.

In sales, there are really just two main things we can develop—how we read and project our body language, and our verbal language. Everything we do is delivered through body language and verbal language. We will go over this in greater detail later.

For the time being, understanding the fact that practices are extremely important is something valuable in itself. It makes us more open to learning and polishing what we should know and understand about selling. Learn more to earn more. Just understand that no matter how much you may know, there is always more to learn—always! By learning more and better practices, we become more efficient and effective.

*In sales, there are really just two main things we can develop—how we read and project our body language, and our verbal language. Everything we do is delivered through body language and verbal language. Great salespeople study sales **and** people!*

Here are a few examples of better practices:

Build Relationships by Being Natural

When you speak with someone on the phone while using a script or word track, you put yourself at an immediate disadvantage. This sales approach doesn't work well for most because it's unnatural. People pick up on the robotic, lifeless feel that comes with reading from a script.

If it is not how you normally talk with your friends, then it shouldn't be utilized in your sales practices. Doing so moves you away from who you really are. And blowing the special opportunity of connecting with someone who is, for the moment, willing to stay on the call will hurt your confidence. If you hear a word track you love, modify and practice it until it becomes you.

With your friends, you speak from the heart—directly from your own mind. It's very natural and spontaneous. Many of your words are memorable and appropriate with the uniqueness of the occasion. It is so natural that you may not even notice that you work towards creating and maintaining a relationship with them.

That is something special that comes from you through the process of communicating this way, and these powerful qualities are nonexistent when reading via a script. It puts the script in-between you and the recipient, dulling the essential qualities and your unique brilliance, which need to be conveyed. Essentially, you become the lifelessness of the script instead of the essence of who you are.

Just think for a moment how unpleasant it is to talk with an automated system. The experience is almost degrading—frustrating at best. Reading from a script is not much different. Study and memorize great word tracks, but use them naturally in your sales conversations.

Be Enjoyable and Interesting in Conversations Over Mobile Devices

Remember that everyone today has caller ID on their cell phones or landlines. Many people avoid talking on the phone, in favor of texting and email, and will screen all calls.

If your client conversations are not perceived as being enjoyable or valuable for them, after one or two calls, your customers will never again pick up the phone when your company name appears on their screen. You do it. I do it. So do your customers. They may not even open or reply to your emails and will ignore your text messages. So please be aware of the detriment that script-related customer conversations can create, as well as robotic contacts that just continually push sales and services, and asking for referrals.

Become Favorably Memorable

Up until the mid-nineties, there was no extensive follow-up system or customer relationship management system in the software business for car dealers, so I developed one.

RelMark Relationship Marketing Software was the very first Windows-based CRM piece in the industry.

We did rather well with the product, putting it in about 400 dealerships in Canada and the United States. The main reason for bringing this up is to validate the fact that I am very adept in CRM, and I understand its value and importance and wish to pass on this knowledge to you.

However, if your idea of Customer Relationship Management is to simply call people when the computer says so and just read the scripts that come with the software, understand that this is short-sided in utilizing the power of this type of system. Know that top salespeople use these systems very differently—to its fullest capacity—and we will discuss this further later on.

Your top salespeople actually create relationships—or REALationships—with their clients after the sale. They know how to make their contacts enjoyable, memorable and valuable after delivery.

Don't Rely on Walk-in Traffic

Walk-in traffic refers to potential customers (prospects) who walk into a showroom, a car lot or a storefront where there are salespeople. A very important point that needs to be stressed is that it's a very bad idea to rely solely on the customer foot traffic of the establishment you work for. This is simply not the way to go if you want to be very successful.

This book will help you move away from this type of reliance on prospects into having more than you know what to do with. You'll have people attracted to you because you'll have made relationships and will be pursuing your business in your "down time" during your "money hours". Pros don't just wait for business; they pursue and attract it as well.

Your day needs to go from waiting to creating!

PSYCHOLOGY

The third P is Psychology. Psychology is how people think and feel. It's universal for the most part and affects both the buyer and seller.

The three words that you need to remember here are: Head, Heart and Gut. Current neuroscience is validating that we actually do some processing and thinking with all three—the head, the heart and the gut.

The "Head" represents the brain and mind—logic from which we make conclusions. The "Heart" is our emotional aspect; how we feel about things. The "Gut" is our intuition; what we sense deep down to our core as being true or false.

Therefore, you need to approach your sales, and life, with these three things in mind, making sure that all three are pulled into the picture during times of indecisiveness. After all, what we are doing as salespeople is persuading people to make a good decision. So, the better you understand your own decision-making processes, the better you will understand your customers'.

So, you need to sell to their Head by supplying information—the details of the product—adequate for making a conclusion through logic.

You need to light up their Heart by touching the emotional aspects of what having the product will fulfill—what the experience of owning the product will be like, how you will treat them after the sale, how it may positively affect friends and family, their image, and so on.

The Gut needs to be dealt with by validating the deeper senses of intuition—what the person believes, who they trust—through things such as honesty, sincerity, and integrity.

Have you ever noticed how good pets and children are when it comes to judging character? They will repel from questionable people and practically jump in the lap of good, kind people. That's the awareness or intuition or "Gut" sense that we all have. They react to the non-verbal cues, and so do many of your customers.

Duane Brain Tip

Reader, it's crucial to be guided by a blueprint of sound Principles which adhere to solid Psychology. With those in hand, creating and following effective Practices is much easier and will ensure that your Patterns of behavior will be aligned in ways to drastically increase your Probability of success.

Head, Heart and Gut Guidance

With these three words in mind, I'd like to share a short story. A friend of mine was going through a fairly major life change and was having difficulties with personal relationships. He was thinking about getting back together with a girlfriend from years ago. He called me up asking for help with this decision, and after a few moments I said, "Let me ask you a couple of quick questions. I need you to answer me as honestly and as quickly as you can. First question is this: out of ten—ten is very good—from your head, what does your logical mind tell you about the long-term possibility of you two working out? What's the first number that comes to your mind?"

He instantly said, "Three."

I said, "Okay, great. What does your heart say about the

long-term prospects or possibilities of this working out for you?"

He said, "Oh my heart's a nine; I just love her."

After that answer, I continued on, "So we've got a three in the head, nine in the heart. Now, the third area is your gut. What does your gut say about this working out?"

He thought for a second and then said, "Maybe a four."

Though you've never met this person, your advice would probably be, "Don't do it."

When faced with a decision, we are capable of thinking and processing information from the head, heart and gut. They can also each trigger their own memories.

Memories of the Heart

A few years ago, while delivering a seminar to a group of salespeople, talking about a very similar analogy with head, heart and gut, a young lady and great salesperson, Sherry, left the room crying. She came back a few minutes later and said, "I want to share a little story with you at lunch."

Her story was that she'd had a heart transplant a few years earlier. After the transplant, she had a compulsion to go downhill skiing. She said, "I had colors of uniforms in my mind, chalets, ski hills, all kinds of stuff, and I'm an equestrian. I love horses and have never skied a day in my life." She could not figure out where this compulsion and desire to ski was coming from. In talking with people from the surgical unit at the hospital, they told her that the heart she received was from a professional skier who actually died while on a ski hill. These sorts of true stories tell us there is a lot going on inside a person, and that we are comprised of much more than we often think.

Do not underestimate the power of your head, heart and your gut, and that of your buyer's. All three need to be sold before a decision can be made.

The Psychology of the Buyer

When in the process of buying something, people process information about the product, you (the salesperson), the company you represent ... through the head, heart and gut. That may be pretty obvious now, but what is also important to realize is that after the sale—when your customers have received the product and you have your commissions—they begin to process information anew, mostly about you—the salesperson—through the same mental and emotional filters. If they question whether or not you were out for their best interests; if they don't feel like you were really giving your all, that you didn't really care about them, or that you will likely not even remember them or care to talk to them now that the sales process is over, you've set yourself up as a target for completely unnecessary strife or struggle.

In other words, if you are not enjoyable, valuable and memorable after the sale, they will not come back to you later for other products, and they certainly won't send you more business by recommending you. Further, they may leave a complaint about you to management. They might even return the product for a refund!

Let's face it, people left to their own devices can let small, negative issues amplify and get out of hand.

Duane Brain Tip

Reader, I will never forget the time when one of my customers recognized that I was tired, under the weather and that I needed a pick-me-up, and he kindly drove me in his car to a Starbucks before my seminar to get a green tea.

Being exhausted and focusing only on myself, I handed him my Starbucks card from the passenger seat, collected my drink, and he drove us off. I didn't ask him if I could buy him something, and I don't even remember thanking him for taking me. It wasn't until later in the day that I realized how rude that unthinking moment must have seemed to him.

We laughed about it when I profusely apologized later. I even mailed him a prepaid Starbucks gift card, but no amount of joking or apologizing could take away the sting of me seeming that cheap or uncaring, and it permanently hurt the relationship. In sales, you only get one chance, and the real sales (and work) start after the first sale.

Creatures of Habit

The other part of this psychology is the fact that we are creatures of habit.

I would like you to please put this book down and cross your arms across your chest—just fold your arms as you naturally would. Now, observe how your arms overlap or intertwine. Which arm or which hand is on top? Study exactly how you fold your arms. Now that you see your natural and comfortable way of folding your arms, I would like you to drop your arms and refold them in the exact opposite way—not different, just opposite (like a mirror image).

I think you'll notice how awkward this feels and how difficult it is; they probably want to unfold and just open up.

My osteopath told me that we begin folding our arms in our most comfortable way in our mother's womb, and that once we develop habits, even simple ones like that, they can be tough to break.

First we make our habits, and then our habits make us.

In life and sales, it is best to control than to be controlled. Choose your habits carefully and get outside of your comfort zone. Use your head, your heart and your gut, and start to create smarter habits. Combine this with focus, purpose, and include proper goals, and you can make significant changes to how well you sell.

PATTERNS

The fourth P is called "Patterns". A high IQ is measured by the ability to notice patterns and then make changes. The world around us is changing rapidly and constantly. If we can't make quick decisions and changes, improvement will be very difficult, and even keeping up with changes will be hard.

So, start to notice what's working and what's not working for yourself and people around you. Once you notice that, you can then start to change undesirable behaviors. This is why it is very important to track important sales metrics so you can notice patterns.

Whatever can be measured can be improved. Things like how many calls, emails, texts and live customers you talked to today, how many presentations and financial proposals you did, your closing ratios, how many of your customers you called, etc. are very important for you to know and track. Remember to be honest with your reporting of sales figures, GIGO (Garbage In, Garbage Out)!

PROBABILITY

The last P is one of the key points of this book, and really what the essence of selling is all about. It is called "Probability". Probability has to do with odds. It's the chances of things happening in certain ways.

For example, the probability of selling EVERY person we meet is zero. Everything that is probable will show itself through the law of large numbers. When you deal with enough people, certain patterns start to show. They are based on your understanding of psychology as well as the practices that you are using and the principles you are following.

If you do many things very well, the probability or odds of selling your client goes up, and if you do things poorly, the odds go down. This should be obvious. If you were to create just a few more leads each month while simultaneously moving your closing ratio up just 10-15%, you could have a combined impact increase of around 30-40% to your overall sales. That is all an effect upon probability.

Duane Brain Tip

Reader, we will all make or miss some sales due to good or bad luck. Sales professionals know the difference between luck and probability, and they realize that things like so-called "fear of rejection" or "fear of the phones" is just misplaced emotions and illogical thinking. Don't fall into the "fear of rejection" lie.

Fear motivates me! I channel my fears properly into the fear of having too much month at the end of my money—the fear of not doing my best; the fear of my children being embarrassed about where or how they live; the fear of not making enough contacts; the fear of not changing with the market, or the fear of losing a sale or my business to a more focused company or salesperson.

Just remember, if you don't change things about yourself, you won't change things for yourself. And even more importantly, if you align your fears properly, they will drive you instead of weaken you.

In Conclusion

By applying the Five Ps to your daily work routine, improvement can occur on a fast track, and you will also ensure ongoing improvements. These are the fundamentals to success. Use them and open the door to greater expansion.

"Too many of us are not living our dreams because we are too busy living our fears."
—*Les Brown*

CHAPTER 2

Committing to Long-Term Success

One of my many goals in this book is to give you more choices. By having more choices in terms of how to think and see things, your mind is expanded. Once expanded, a mind can never really contract to where it was before. I'm not here to tell you what to do, how to behave or how you must sell, but through a little patience, some reading and keeping notes, you will have dozens of new choices and ideas on how you can deal with your clients and your profession in better ways.

Long-Term Perspective

When the term "career" is referred to, you should have a long-term mindset about it. When you approach your endeavor with a long-term commitment, and not just as a short-term job, your work ethic and processes will take on a more beneficial slant. You deal with problems and challenges in a completely different way, and you study and learn willingly, with more excitement.

Business vs. "Busyness"

Let's take a look at the word *business*. We're all in business. Whatever you put into your entrepreneurial spirit that you bring with you to work everyday is really going to affect your income and where you're going. You usually have the support mechanisms of the company—computer systems, training, technicians that maintain your product, the inventory that someone else stocks for you to sell, the advertising, the location and their reputation. Hence, you're in business for yourself, but not by yourself. At the end of the day, you have all those resources available to you, and you get to turn them into something for yourself through your selling skills.

I find that it's difficult to work on your business in the middle of the "busyness" of it all. During your money-making hours, you are actively taking and making calls, dealing with confrontation and opposition, meeting customers, attending meetings, and dozens of other things that readily present themselves to you.

"Learn to focus on what's important, not just what's urgent."

—*Stephen Covey*

Those things are urgent in the short term but possibly not as important, long term, as some of the things we will be talking about in this book that, once mastered, can increase your business many times over.

For example, most people never finish reading books that they start or use gym memberships they pay for because they feel they are too busy and that it isn't urgent.

Simply put, don't be average. Finish what you start.

I advise you to read this book with a pen or highlighter in hand so you can highlight certain areas and make notes in the column. Or maybe keep an additional notepad beside you so you can look back at key points and refresh your mind quickly and efficiently.

A JOB vs. an MBA

If you go to work everyday and treat your work like a job, you will only have just that—a JOB—(or be *Just Over Broke)* because you won't be putting your all into it. You'll exert just enough energy to keep your job. I know, because I've had lots of "just jobs" in the past. You will know if your current work is "just a job" for you if you have this internal dialogue that says something like: *Why am I working so hard for this?* or *Oops, I better work a little bit harder before my boss sees me!* With this kind of approach, your goal is only to keep that job or paycheck, and nothing more. But in sales, minimal effort (and skills) equals minimal sales (and pay). And such a lifeless goal as this will offer no drive whatsoever for improvement, excellence or success.

"Sales is either the best-paying full-time job or the worst-paying part-time job!"
—*Tom Hopkins*

With this kind of approach, your goal is only to keep that job or paycheck, and nothing more. But in sales, minimal effort (and skills) equals minimal sales (and pay). And such a lifeless goal as this will offer no drive whatsoever for improvement, excellence or success.

If a simple, unattached job is not the answer to more income and a higher standard of living, how about getting an MBA? I'm not referring to the usual Master of Business Administration that we're accustomed to. Interestingly enough, no formal education or background is necessarily required to be successful in many entrepreneurial ventures. You can enter into these things with nothing except a good attitude and a willingness to learn. Those skills, along with the desire to improve and help your customers while making money, can result in you having an MBA, or a "Massive Bank Account."

So, what determines whether you have a JOB (Just Over Broke) or an MBA, (Massive Bank Account)? Your selling skills. The best part is that you have 100% control over your skills, and, based on your imagination, experiences and information, you can improve them.

Be careful of what you study. Just because something is (or was) popular doesn't make it right for today's climate. Statements like, "Stay away from the price of the product," "Slow the prospect down," or "Follow up your customers" aren't necessarily appropriate. We will talk more about these later.

The point is, you could be studying stale or incorrect information, and, if so, you're going to get a result, but maybe not the result you're hoping for. Mastering a bad technique is a bad idea. You have to make sure that you're studying the right information for today's world and for the brand that you're selling, in the market you're selling it, and for the management and ownership whom you are selling it with.

The other difference between a JOB and MBA is how much you love what you do. If you love what you do, and if you really care about your clients, your brand, your own future, or if you love anything else that is related to the goals that you want to achieve for yourself or somebody else, you can move from "just over broke" to a "massive bank account" because it's all going to be based on what you put into your endeavor.

If you're like most people, you are probably suffering from a vitamin L deficiency (more on this in the Six Powers chapter). We all want to give and get a little more LOVE. Find some things that you can fall in love with about your career, and you could be finding the missing link between your JOB and your MBA.

A Trade vs. a Profession

My father had to leave his hometown in Pola, Italy before it became Yugoslavia (now part of Croatia and renamed Pula). That part of Italy was lost in WW2, and my father, at fourteen years of age, had the choice to stay and become a communist in Yugoslavia, or leave. He decided to leave.

Even though my mother is known as Phyllis, her first name is really Filomena. During and after WW2, anyone of Italian decent had an awfully hard time, so she had to recreate herself just to find work or finish school. The way of the world is adapt, or die.

When my father left Italy, he had already lost his brother and hero Alfredo. His parents had lost their home, their business, and his neighborhood was decimated. He ended up in refugee camps for three years until he came to Canada at seventeen years of age. It's a fairly typical immigrant story for which I have the utmost respect. I can't even imagine having to go through that struggle—as many of you, your family and friends have done—to improve yourself. So, when someone talks about drive, immigrants understand drive. That drive is usually part of why they're here because they're looking to improve themselves.

My father bounced around jobs until he was about twenty-one or twenty-two, doing whatever he could to survive. I know many of us have been in that situation before.

He ultimately became a machinist, and when he got those papers, he got a trade. (My mother actually wrote his test answers for him as he couldn't read or write English yet.)

As my father said many times, he never looked back, and he never had to worry about employment again because he had that trade. He then made the daily decision to improve his trade, continually. My father loved how the engineers with all the letters after their names would often consult him to fix their problems. A few of his solutions even ended up being patented.

The difference between a trade and a profession is that the trade really gives you a skill set that you can bring anywhere. Plumbers, electricians, bricklayers, sheet metal workers all have trades. People with great trades and a great reputation are never worried about employment because there is always a bigger demand for their skills than there is a supply, and it gives them a huge employment advantage.

Some professions, on the other hand, can involve a pro-longed indoctrination process, which, in the end, may actually limit you because of its narrow employment appli-cations within your organization.

In this way, I feel a professional sales career is actually a skilled trade. One thing about being in sales, especially car sales, is that once you develop a high skill set and maintain a great reputation, you'll never worry about unemployment again. The demand for your skill set with customers and dealerships (or any company) always has been and always will be higher than the supply. So, the one thing you can count on if you master your trade is that you will never worry about being out of work again, and this is especially true for outstanding retail automotive sales professionals.

Duane Brain Tip

Reader, there is always an undersupply of great people in the business world because the ownership and management teams always want to improve their volume and profits, not to mention keep the lights on and phones ringing by having their bills paid. As true capitalists and entrepreneurs, they want to sell more products and make more money, and they know that highly-skilled salespeople with great character and credibility allow them to do that. Even if you have to move, if you're skilled, there's always a position for you somewhere. All companies need salespeople, but hopefully you would not want or need to move as there are pitfalls of moving that we will take up later in the book.

To get a better grip on this, let's imagine that you go to work, and your name is Leo Chang. On your office door, it says, "Leo Chang, CEO". Every morning that you go to work, you have accountability to yourself because you are the owner of your own business. Within legal, ethical and company parameters, you have the right to say where and how you spend your time, your money, what records you keep, how you manage and maintain your own customer base, and you know the level of skill you have in selling or presenting your products to customers. You want to get a good return on your investment (ROI) as well as a good return on your energy (ROE). If you do this, there will be success for both you and your company.

Ways to Get Out of a Job

I was repossessing cars a number of years ago, in my early twenties. One of my first mentors in business was a man named Rick, and I'm not really sure if he even knows he was a mentor. Rick had asked me, "Duane, you really don't want to be doing this forever, do you?"

I said, "No, Rick, I don't."

It was a corporate job. I was just finishing up my university degree after working at a Chrysler dealership that closed, and I thought I was in-between jobs. He had recognized that I really didn't want to do this for a career.

He said, "Well, I can see you don't want to do this forever, but now you have a bit of a problem on your hands."

I said, "What's the problem?"

"The problem is there's only three ways to get out of a job that you don't like."

And I responded with, "Really, Rick, what's that?" He was older than I, probably by about fifteen years and had a quirky kind of country wisdom about him. I had an open mind, and I was listening; I liked the man.

He said, "Well, the first way out of a job is to get promoted. A lot of businesses or companies have a structure that allows you to get promoted within the company. But the opportunity for promotion will likely never come up unless you give your current job 100%. The last thing your bosses want is to bring up some dead weight to their own level that they'd now have to carry. So, Duane, unless you give something 100%, you're never going to get promoted.

"Second way is this: you can get out of the job you've got by repeats and referrals. Grow your demand and value within the business or job you're at. Your current bosses or customers like you so much, and, because you're doing such a great job, they send you even more work. Or it starts to come from their friends, family, coworkers, or associations. A repeat or a referral is really an acknowledgement from an existing customer that you're doing an outstanding job. But you're not going to get a lot of repeats and referrals unless your customer base—the people you've been dealing with internally or externally—believes that you've been giving them 100%. Nobody will send their friends and family to someone they don't like, respect or trust."

"What's the third way?"

"The third way is through getting headhunted—getting hired away. You have to recognize that people are always watching you (and with today's technology, could be recording you!) If they see excellence, they may want it for themselves in their own businesses."

Both of my children received soccer scholarships—my daughter in Louisiana, and my son in Iowa—and one of the things I told them, along with the other players on their teams when I was one of their trainers, is that you never know who's watching you. Everyone has audio and video recorders on their smartphones (or as I like to say, "Their mobile computers that they happen to talk into occasionally!")

I know that when coaches watch games, they're also watching to see your attitude and how you are in the pregame conversations—how you talk to your parents and other players, how respectful you are to the coach, what you treat the referee like. You're always being watched. That awareness was one of the advantages they had when the scouts came to watch.

Similarly, at work, you're always being watched, and you don't know who's watching you. But you're not going to get headhunted (or stolen) unless the people who are watching you are blown away (in a good way) by what you're doing. If they see what you're doing and they love what they see, they may come up and say, "Hey, excuse me, I love your work. If you're not happy doing what you're doing now with this company, I'd love to hire you. Here's my business card. Get in touch with me."

Duane Brain Tip

Reader, know that your customers will often use their technology to do the same—watch you. It's not unusual for your buyer to take pictures of everything on your desk when you leave the room, snapshots of your computer screen and record voice notes of your conversations. Be wise and be careful. Work on all your deals within a folder, and, when leaving your desk, close the folder and put it to one side. Also, be sure to minimize or turn off your computer screen when leaving your office.

"So, Duane, you won't get headhunted; you won't get repeats or referrals; you won't get a promotion, and, unless you give it 100%, you will be stuck here forever."

I can literally remember what the weather was like outside when Rick told me that, and it struck me like a lightening bolt on top of my head. I could not argue with him; what he had said was logical and made sense. I made a commitment from that day forward to start giving 100%, and that was the beginning of my professional turnaround.

With that same company, I took several promotions and became influential on a national scale. I also learned some of the same skill sets I use to run my business today. My upward movement and national exposure within that company would never have happened if I hadn't started to give it 100%—when I didn't like what I was doing! I have to suppress laughing out loud when I hear salespeople say, "I'll start to give it my all when I start to make more money!" This is completely backwards.

Rick told me another thing. He said, "All communities and customers interact with each other on some level."

There's a book out there called, *Six Degrees of Separation*. The author talks about how, through about six people, we are connected to everybody on the planet, but the theory of that book was really written before the Internet. And I'll tell you, between Facebook, Twitter, LinkedIn, Pinterest, all the social websites, emails, text messaging, recording, and the sharing technology we have, I don't believe in six degrees of separation anymore. It's now more like two degrees of separation! We can get ourselves in front of anybody we want right now because of technology.

So, here's my warning to you: don't step on anybody's toes because they may be connected to the same bum you might have to kiss one day.

Duane Brain Tip

Reader, along the same vein, most of us know a few hundred people. Everyone has at least 100 Facebook friends; so, if a post is shared by just 10 of your 100 friends, 1,000 people may "know" you in a matter of moments. This fact can make or break you in a very big way.

So it's important, more than ever, to protect your reputation and your online presence like your career depends on it—because it really does.

Any diligent human resource manager will "Google" and "Facebook" a potential new hire, and so will most of your customers. Is your online presence saying what you think it should for maximum professional face value? An aggravated customer can do serious harm online, and professional death by Google and social media is not fun. Google your own name regularly, and deal with problems and heat scores as soon as you can.

That was some of the best advice I had ever been given and at the right time—especially because the car business is a huge business, but it is very small at the same time. I imagine most industries are the same in that way.

I know for sure that not everyone loves me. I've offended a few people at seminars doing what I do passionately, and not everyone appreciates my straight-up approach, as I'm always respectful, but I can be pretty direct and truthful. I've also made tens of thousands of people extremely happy and more successful by passing on what I have learned and lived. My intentions are always good, and I have never purposely gone out and burned bridges. I've never intentionally stepped on any toes; I've never willingly taken advantage of anybody. I'm no saint, but I sleep very well at night. So, if you are used to stepping on toes or think it's a way to get ahead, just know, as I said earlier, they may be connected to the same bum you will have to eventually kiss.

I can tell you that on more than one occasion, during a

sale, a meeting or a presentation, I looked around the room and realized that there was somebody there who would be influential to my outcome that day. That same somebody might have said or done something I didn't agree with years earlier, and I just thanked my lucky stars that I never did anything on purpose to burn that bridge because he or she is now a decision maker and could negatively affect me. I always try to make amends or at least state my case politely as to why I did what I did so that I'm not stepping on any toes. I learned that thanks to Rick and his great advice.

Duane Brain Tip

Reader, be careful, while you are trying to not step on any toes, that you don't make the next biggest mistake of trying to be everything to everyone, because you will really end up being nothing to most. Be yourself, and just keep your intentions and integrity intact.

In Conclusion

Your trade as a salesperson requires you to be efficient, effective, well trained and up-to-date. Make the decision to be in it for the long run, or find a new line of work. It makes no sense to keep faking it or wasting time doing something you really don't want to do. Give 100% to everything you do—from learning to skill building to customer service. This will get you out of your JOB and into an MBA.

CHAPTER 3

Performance Psychology

Let's continue on with something called Performance Psychology. Here, psychology is loosely defined as the mental or emotional factors affecting a situation or activity. Performance Psychology affects how you perform.

There are so many ways I could approach this concept, but as starting points, do you generally stay within your comfort zones, or do you try new things? How do you learn to be successful? Do you learn by making mistakes or by copying other successful people? What prerequisites do you need in order for you to grow and improve as an individual? How can you recognize what will work for you?

"Life is too short to take the long way to your goals."

—*Tony Robbins*

Simply put, after training and coaching tens of thousands of people, I feel the majority of successes (or failures) are due to one's psychological approach while only a small amount are due to actual strategy. In this chapter, we will take a look at some ways we can affect our neurology and psychology to become more successful.

Understanding success and performance psychology can go a long way towards cutting down the time it takes you to become successful. It can also help you make fewer mistakes and put you on the path to getting what you want in this life. One of the major points in the fact-based movie *Rush* was that Niki Lauda's difference—that made the difference for him—was his deep understanding of the machine he was driving. In the same spirit, understanding more about how you are wired can help you tremendously.

Success leaves a lot of clues. Meeting so many salespeople, I can tell you that most successful salespeople do a lot of similar things even though most of them have never met or heard of each other. And, in addition, failure leaves clues that we can learn from. All people, including ourselves, are either examples or lessons.

Personal Set Points or Comfort Zones

If I set my house thermostat at 72 degrees, it does not hold a constant 72 degrees. This would be the average temperature—one that the system is going to try to maintain. Different areas of the room will be hotter or colder, but what happens throughout the day is that it will cycle around 72 degrees as its medium or average. So it might go up to 74 degrees before the air conditioning kicks in, or it might dip to 70 degrees before the heater kicks in. But you will notice that your air conditioner or heater, depending on what season it is, will turn off and on during the day as it tries to maintain an average comfort zone of its 72 degree set point. We tend to stay within several psychological comfort zones too.

Success leaves a lot of clues ... All people, including ourselves, are either examples or lessons.

Financial Comfort Zone or Set Point

One of those comfort zones deals with our finances.

Using a thermostat as an analogy to demonstrate, let's stretch that 72 degrees out into a hypothetical number of $72,000. Maybe your comfort zone is making $72,000 a year. For some people, it may be $72,000 a month. That is their comfort zone of what they need or want to make. So, whatever it is, make a note of it now.

First question: how did you come to that amount as your financial comfort zone or set point? Where did this number come from? Did it come from society, friends, family members, coworkers, what you made at your last job, or what your parents made? Does it come from what you feel you need to make per month, or is it an amount you need to pay your bills? Does that number include enough to buy an income property or retirement savings, or pay for your kids' college? Did it come from what you want or what you need to make now, in the future, or what you made in the past?

My point is, your desired annual or monthly income number is extremely arbitrary; we usually adopt it subconsciously from various sources around us.

Nonetheless, using $72,000 as an example, let's break this down into an average of $6,000 per month. As an entrepreneur or commissioned salesperson, your income is most likely going to go up and down throughout the year, and hopefully you will have made your average of $72,000 by the end of the year. Let's imagine then that some months you make $3,000 or $4,000, and other months you make $8,000 or $9,000.

Let's say a few months go by, and you make below your desired average. One month, you make $5,000; the next month, $4,800, followed by $5,100 and $3,200. Obviously, you're not making what you should be making.

There are two common reactions. An unaware person might not even notice that his or her income has been sliding for the last few months and therefore does nothing differently to stop the slide.

Another person notices right away after a few days or a couple of weeks and creates changes to turn things around before it becomes a disaster. Just based on that, which person do you predict will be more successful?

The acutely aware person is going to be in a better position to turn it around quicker before it becomes disastrous. Another thing to notice here is how differently people behave when they see their income sliding.

Some people start blaming everybody else. As soon as they notice the drop, they may start to blame the receptionist. "The receptionist must be giving the leads to somebody else when no one's looking." Or they'll blame the sales manager or their inventory. They'll blame the advertising as being ineffective. "The product must be lapsing. The competitor must have a better promotion." Perhaps they blame the phone system, their computers, location or weather. These people will blame everybody except themselves.

But when a person notices his situation too late, or he blames everybody else for his lack of prospects or sales, the next step is often a bad case of G.I.A.G.O.T.O.S. (grass is always greener on the other side syndrome) and start calling around looking for another job.

This person is smart enough to drop their negative attitudes during the job interviews at the other store, usually creating some story that their new potential managers will find empathy or sympathy in, say all the right things, and get by unsuspecting, naive, hopeful or lazy managers who are hoping they are walking into a lucky catch.

Of course, when he or she quits for greener pastures, they will often find out that the game is the same; only the players are different. Worse yet, they will have left behind their power base—their customers. And typically, as soon as they pass their probation, their work ethic and attitude will regress back to what it really is—"special" as I call it—and resume being caustic haters of anything and everyone who may try to improve or change them.

This special person likely has a pretty low EQ (emotional quotient). If you go online and take an EQ test, you will be able to see the factors that affect your EQ. Unlike IQ (intelligence quotient), which is, for the most part, quite static through your life, your EQ score will change throughout. You may also want to consider your OQ (openness quotient) score. This is simply a measurement of how open you are to new ideas. Remember, for things to change for you, it's logical that things need to change about you. The mark of a truly intelligent person is the ability to entertain any thought without judging it; including that you may be the cause of your problems! Most successful people have average IQs, and very high EQs and OQs. The best news is that your EQ and OQ are totally within your control and ability to change right now!

I will leave these ideas with you as something you may want to further research and Google on your own.

Now, let's have a look at the reactions people have to their income when it is going up. This will be a different scenario. What happens when, instead of making $6,000 a month on average, you're making $7,000-$10,000 a month? Do you view that as just luck? Or do you see it as the result of some current economic situation, the market, or season? Do you look for clues and evidence as to what great things you've been doing to create this momentum?

What you do when your income increases will depend upon whether you think it's luck or something you've done to cause the increase.

I have noticed that there are also two typical patterns that a lot of people fall into when they make more money than expected.

One pattern is that some salespeople or commission-based individuals will start showing up to work late and leaving early. They take and make fewer phone calls and stop sending out or responding to texts and emails as they should, or even stop returning people's messages altogether. They'll take a few sick days off or some vacation days. They don't feel the need to talk to as many walk-ins, and they stop doing their own deliveries. And, of course, their level of productivity, sales and income will start to drop significantly.

Naturally, because they stopped doing the activities that caused the increase in sales, they inevitably cause their income to drop again! And only when they're on the absolute bottom of an income slide, and it becomes totally unbearable, do they start to work hard again by engaging in more positive behaviors and productive activities, dedicating more time to tasks that are focused on their sales. This is a losing battle of self-sabotage—a vicious circle. It's a roller coaster to nowhere and will bring eventual failure, burn out, or both.

Then there's the second pattern, which involves the type of salesperson who is more sensitive to the rises and falls of income and takes on the responsibility for any drops as well as increases. Such salespeople tend to notice quickly (before much money is lost) when things are not going the way they want. When things are on an upswing, this

type will quickly try to notice what was done to cause the upswing and start to do those actions even more.

> *"Am I doing the most productive thing possible right now?"*
>
> —*Tom Hopkins*

They will continue to do more of the most productive activities, and try to push even more of an upswing in income because they know that business has seasons and that they should make hay while the sun shines. And, of course, what they do with it after they make it is an entirely different thing!

All of this is part of the comfort zone or personal set point I call your "financial comfort zone". This is an area that we would do well to understand intimately, pay attention to and work on.

Knowing What Your Time Zone is

Here is a question to ponder: how time sensitive are you with your own productive sales activities?

Previously, I asked you about your financial comfort zone: how much money per month or per year do you need to make? How do you behave when you make less or more than expected? Do you take full accountability for your own income or do you act "special" and blame everyone and everything but yourself?

For your personal "time zone", try to determine how long you can go without talking to a prospect or a buyer before feeling uneasy, anxious, uncomfortable … How much time needs to go by before you feel that you have to take some action and put somebody in front of you, or get a prospect on the phone or send a business text or email?

Some salespeople can go much longer without talking to prospects and buyers than others. Many average and below average salespeople have very long time zones early in the month as they feel they have weeks to pull it together, and those same salespeople are often overly relaxed after a good sale or two and feel no need to seek out a fresh customer right away.

For the highly time-sensitive, short time-zoned sales professionals and angels, they are working just as hard to sell on the 2nd of the month as they are on the 28th, and after a sale, they are immediately trying to welcome or cultivate new business. Those people who are more time sensitive— more intolerant of down time—like to be busy finding prospects and filling up their appointment calendars all the time (more on this later). It's another way of understanding where they are headed and a good indication that they are heading toward success.

So, ask yourself, how long can you go without some sales activity before you get anxious?

Emotional Comfort Zone or Set Point

Our third set point or comfort zone is called an "emotional comfort zone". We are creatures of habit because we like to be emotionally comfortable. Everything we do right now, from the way we brush our teeth and cross our arms to how we greet people and handle objections … everything we do on a regular basis was initially uncomfortable for us when we were first learning how to do them. Things are uncomfortable when we are not used to them, but once we do them a few times, they become second nature to us. But we can get caught into the traps and limitations of our own emotional comfort zones and stop trying new things.

If you look at your emotional comfort zone and your tolerance for doing things that are uncomfortable for you, here's another thing you will notice: successful people have goals and an idea of where they want to go. They'll notice that their financial plans and situations are or are not exactly what they want right now, and they'll notice which way it is trending. They'll also notice how they spend their time and whether or not the amount of time they invest does or does not line up with their financial or sales productivity goals.

They are willing to engage in things that are uncomfortable for them if it helps them grow in areas that are related to the attainment of their goals. They will step outside of their comfort zones and do whatever it takes to get to that goal.

The reality is that if you do the same things but want different results, it's not likely to happen.

To understand that, you have to look at the difference between result goals and activity goals. Result goals are the things you say you want to have happen. Activity goals are the things you are actually doing to get there. At the end of the month, your results are the sum total of the activities you are or are not doing.

In conclusion of this section regarding how you deal with your time, financial set points, and emotional comfort zones, it would be wise for you to increase your sensitivity and awareness for a while regarding how you spend your time, your behavior and attitudes relative to your income, and how you react when pushed outside your emotional comfort zones. And then make efforts to shape yourself in these areas in ways that make sense to you.

Exercise

Identify how you behave when you make more or less money than expected. How do you react? Do you go into denial? Do you work less, or do you work harder? Do you look at yourself for causes, or do you just blame others for your results? I can tell you from my involvement in many sports that it is very common for parents and players to blame the referee, the weather, the coach and faulty playing conditions rather than to admit they played poorly!

Notice how you spend your time. What percentage of your day or how many hours a day are you truly productive? As a parent, I have seen my children spend hours doing everything but studying the day before a test, and I often did the same at their age. Are you productive outside of work? In sales, all your hours could be your money hours if used wisely.

Lastly, how do you feel and act when you're doing things that are emotionally uncomfortable for you? Do you shy away from them or grab the bull by the horns? Doing targeted things that are more productive, although uncomfortable, is smart. Like a muscle, if you don't use it, you will lose it. I try to remember to stay "comfortably uncomfortable" by trying new and better things all the time in many areas of my life.

In Conclusion

There are many things I currently do and love that at one time were new and uncomfortable to me, whether it's in my relationships, athletics, real estate, diet, personal and business finances, sales processes, speaking engagements, or things that relate to my family and friends.

Remaining comfortable with your current processes carries with it the assumption that things will stay the same, but in life and business, this is a serious oversight of reality. Everything is impermanent. The cost of living, competition, the value of the dollar, the economy, inflation … things are changing all the time, so there is a constant necessity to grow and improve from where you are today even if you want to stay the same.

And remember, the only competition that really matters is you! Every day, get up with the goal of becoming a little better than your younger you was yesterday. Never be jealous of success, just be genuinely curious as to how those who are successful did it; and once you figure that out, do it yourself.

CHAPTER 4

Shortcuts to Success

What other shortcuts to success are available to us? A lot of our potential has to do with the methods we adopt to grow and develop our skills, habits and attitudes. Fundamentally, there are really only three ways that we learn and build skills.

Learning by Experience

The first method of learning is through something we're all familiar with—experience. Learning through experience is slow, subjective, and often fraught with unnecessary errors. Your ability to learn solely through the lens of your own experiences will always be limited in time and scope as it can only draw from a very finite body of knowledge.

As individuals, we are often not exposed to enough situations over a sufficiently compressed timespan to be able to develop a permanent skill set through personal trial and error alone.

So, while personal experience is very important, and some people will proudly tell you they have "been in the business" for twenty years or more (which is great), people will sometimes just repeat what they learned in their first year of business for the next nineteen years and never really experience a high level of professional growth.

If you've been in a line of business for five years and haven't noticed any real, tangible improvements in your results, you've probably repeated your first year five times over. That isn't really a shortcut to success; in fact, that's the long road.

Experience without growth will also have you just repeating all of the same sales steps over and over. And when you're dealing with customers in a changing market, you might not want to follow every step each time. For angels, each sale is as different as their individual customers.

We know, for example, that the Internet has modified our customers' buying processes tremendously; yet, in many cases, sales processes remain unchanged from 20 years ago. When someone comes in who is already closed on your product, but you insist on being "thorough" by pedantically forcing them through all the steps of your two-hour sales cycle, chances are you could actually lose a sale that was handed to you on a silver platter. Forcing the full process on every customer could cause many transaction ready customers to unravel and *not* buy out of frustration. You can absolutely talk yourself out of a sale if you don't understand how and when to take a shortcut to the sale with the right customer.

You can absolutely talk yourself out of a sale if you don't understand how and when to take a shortcut to the sale with the right customer.

Duane Brain Tip

Reader, if someone comes in already sold, you just need to confirm you have the right product and then you complete the transaction. In such a case, the product orientation is given on delivery.

Twenty or more years ago, we wanted to slow down the sale and for a very good reason: without the Internet, customers had to physically go from store to store for even basic information. So, after two hours or more into the sales process, the buyer would realize that if they left without buying, they would have to start all over at another dealership. In avoidance of this, they would buy what we were selling and pay us what we wanted.

Nowadays, A.G. (After Google), our experience shows us that our fastest sales can often be our most profitable while also resulting in the most referrals! If a prospect comes in already sold and we transact the sale quickly and smoothly, making it easy on them, they will appreciate it and might even pay us a little more to reciprocate the great service!

Successful salespeople (and business people in general) don't skip steps, speed things up, or slow things down. Instead, they treat each sales cycle as a unique event and focus on the individual FLOW of each sale. In fact, my own sales processes, which are trademarked, are called FLOW Selling, both in F&I (finance and insurance) and in sales.

If you can get something done in 20 minutes instead of two hours, especially if it is more effective, why wouldn't you? If an angel can close a customer in thirty minutes instead of an hour and a half, you can bet he or she will.

Later in this book, I will cover multiple ways of identifying whether you're looking at a ten-minute sale or whether the customer will require the full process.

The average transaction time to buy a car used to be over 2 hours, and today, with FLOW Selling, it's about 45 minutes. If your customers are slowed down or left alone, unentertained, they immediately return to their cell phones or tablets (and you are losing control), as well as become agitated or bored and come up with objections. More FLOW equals more dough! Keep things moving!

Learning by Trial and Error

Trial and error is a learning method that should go hand in hand with experience. While you are experiencing things, you should always be alert to identifying any errors you make and figuring out how to correct them on the spot for the next time around. This study should happen on missed sales as well as successful ones so that every day, in any way, you are getting a little better.

When you identify things that don't work and try new things to obtain better results, that's learning by trial and error. We all know someone who never seems to show any substantial improvements in their career through increased sales or income, improved sales metrics, reduced stress or reduced time to sell. In spite of having many years of experience, these individuals are not applying the method of trial and error because they have stopped testing and adapting long ago. Very often, they are in a rut, and because they've been in it for so long, they don't even know it.

Conversely, if there were ways to avoid some errors completely while taking full advantage of other people's experiences, who wouldn't want to do that? This is the core concept behind the third learning method, called *modeling*.

Learning by Modeling

Simply put, modeling means replicating or emulating what other people do. Human beings are natural modelers. We pick up our language, our eating habits, our beliefs and values in life, our body language, behaviors, and even opinions from our friends and family around us. This is why it is so important that you choose whom you spend your time with very carefully and pick people to model yourself after rather than leaving it up to random luck or proximity to influence your choices. Choose carefully whom you are going to copy.

Here are the fundamentals to modeling or copying success:

First, you have to decide what you want. Perhaps you want to pay your house off sooner (Kevin C.), to be more physically fit (Mike B.), to be a better closer in sales (Ron G.), or maybe you want to handle phone calls better (Doug S.) Really, it can be anything that is important to you.

(Note: thank you to the names in the parentheses because you were my primary models who helped me to start achieving excellence in all of those areas, and you didn't even know it at the time!)

Once you have decided what you want, the next step is to look around for companies and people that are getting the results you want for yourself. You want to look for things that work and for people who do very, very well in those areas.

Maybe you find something in a book, a CD, a course of study, or a workshop. Perhaps the successful person is someone famous, or someone you work with, a neighbor or even someone in your own family. When you're modeling, you're modeling specific traits and not the entire person. Nobody is perfect, so don't throw the baby out with the bathwater. Even average salespeople in your company may be very good at some particular thing.

Stop being judgmental or jealous, and start becoming curious about how people get the results they get. There have been many people in my life that I've modeled in certain areas. There are things about them that I may not like or respect, but in a certain area, I absolutely love what they've done and what they do. I copy that area of their business or individual life plan and incorporate it into my own.

Once you research and discover their successful actions, the next thing to do is duplicate exactly what they've done. This means you will have to get out of your own habitual comfort zones.

Modeling success is much less painful than trial and error, and much faster than learning through experience.

Allow me to give you an example. If you want to learn how to make a fantastic pizza, you can do it through your own experience or trial and error, and end up wasting a lot of time and money; or you can find someone who makes what you consider to be a great pizza, spend time in their kitchen, make note of everything they are doing, and then just copy the entire process. And because you've witnessed it with your own eyes and tasted it, you obviously believe it's a great recipe. What you are doing is modeling their success and taking advantage of their years of trials, errors and experiences. You're coming in after it's all been figured out. What a fantastic way to get to success!

Modeling is the best way by far to quickly come to know ideal procedures and traits for yourself. Drop your ego, admit you don't know it all, start looking for people who do parts of your sales processes better than you, and just commit to copying them! Why waste time reinventing the wheel when you don't have to?

What do you Study?

If you want to be a lawyer, you have to study law and the changes to laws. If you want to be an accountant, you have to study accounting and tax law changes. And if you want to become a better salesperson, you have to study sales and people and how they are changing.

Question: would you rather learn from someone who was a lawyer 20 years ago, or from someone who is successfully practicing law today? This is why I have made a commitment to continue selling cars while being a sales trainer. Things change, and I keep changing with them.

Some of you reading this have seen me personally deal with customers and work the phones, emails and texts at your dealership. That's right—I walk the talk. If you're interested in having me do that for you while I'm training at your store, just ask.

After Joe Girard called me, I had his son Joe Girardi Jr., who also sells cars very successfully, come watch me work the phones and sell cars at a nearby Ford dealership for three days (the full story is on my website). As a result of the skills, work ethic, attitude and results that I demonstrated to his son, I was then able to lock down a meeting with Joe Girard himself. I would have never invited his son to watch me in action with customers if I had doubted my real-world skills as a salesperson.

Product knowledge will come, and this, too, is part of success. You probably have the tools, computer systems and other individuals immediately available to you to help you if you have a problem with your product knowledge. But if you can't figure that buyer out, if you are unable to relate to the buyer, or if you just don't know a sales technique to help you in a particular situation, this lack of knowledge will absolutely cost you many sales.

So, like the lawyer who enjoys studying law and precedents, hopefully you'll enjoy studying sales and people. This book is really a brief study of sales and people, focusing around our six primary sales powers. These six powers will be taken up more fully, shortly. Before we go into this, however, one important thing we should look at is the difference between a salesperson and a person just in sales.

A Salesperson vs. Someone in Sales

If you are sitting in a restaurant and overhear someone talking about buying a product that you sell, what do you do?

Hopefully, you reach into your pocket without a second thought and pull out one of your business cards. A salesperson knows that an opportunity can come around at any point in time, and it can become more difficult to create an opportunity for yourself if you don't have any cards with you. Therefore, the first step to any potential lead is having your cards (and smartphone!) on you.

Before leaving that restaurant, a real salesperson would feel compelled to make sure that person is given an opportunity to get to know him or her. It may seem like a small thing, but a simple thing like leaving home without business cards may be an indication that you consider yourself just a person in sales, rather than a salesperson.

If for some reason a salesperson didn't have cards on her, she would not allow this to stop her. A salesperson would write her name and number on a napkin, walk over and, with a quirky smile, politely say something like, "Hi, I don't want to bother you, and I wasn't eavesdropping, but the restaurant got a little bit quiet there for a moment, and I overheard you saying that you might be looking for a _____. You know what? It's kind of crazy, but that's exactly what I sell. Here's my name and number and where I work … you never know.…"

You might then pause for a second and observe whether there is interest or not for further discussion. As the case may be, you would either supply more information as requested, or graciously return to your table.

If you left that restaurant without passing a card or at least a napkin, and if you didn't walk over and didn't care, you might just be a person in sales rather than a salesperson. A person who is just in sales will always play the sales game with less intensity than a person who sees himself as a true salesperson.

Growth and Improvement Prerequisites

There are three abilities we need to have in place before we can even start to improve ourselves:

1. RECOGNIZE: we have to have the skill to rapidly identify what works and what doesn't. "Scotoma" is a word which loosely means "blind spot". Have you ever gone into the fridge and been unable to find the milk or the ketchup that you know is there, and you don't see it no matter how hard you look? Just as you're ready to swear that it's gone, someone else walks over and pulls it right out from the front and center of the fridge.

Similarly, have you ever lost your keys, and it turned out they were in your pocket or even in your hand?

My nephew is a police officer, and he is often at accident scenes. The first thing people will tell him is, "It's not my fault," followed by, "I didn't see them." How is it that we are unable to see something that is right in front of us? The theories behind it are less important than how we deal with it when it comes to sales.

You can get into a car accident or even lose your life if you don't see things, so the destructive power of blind spots should not be underestimated.

You probably have someone you know who makes the same mistakes over and over in their life. You may have even sat down with them and tried to get them to see what they were doing and what they could do better. If you're talking to them about a personal blind spot they have, you will see their eyes glaze over as they look off in the distance, almost as if they're going into a trance. The area that is giving them all their problems is obscured by a huge blind spot. They really can't see it, so they can't improve it or may feel that the required change would be more painful than the problem itself.

It's very important to illuminate the blind spots in your business and business plan to the best of your ability. Like the refrigerator example, it may require the help of others. While you could elicit the help of friends and family for your personal matters, you need to work with an expert in your field to help you identify sales-related blind spots. Also, know that there are people out there such as myself or your management team who can offer helpful insights simply by having a different perspective than your own. Just like in sports, the coach always sees different things than the players do. So be willing to hear what anyone has to say in helpful criticism as long as their intentions are sincere and not ill-willed.

We all develop blind spots. Step out and analyze yourself from an external perspective as though you are looking at someone else, and do this often.

To help with the elimination of blind spots, we do

case studies at my sales manager workshops around the most successful sales managers and dealerships to identify how the attendees' dealerships are the same and how they differ.

"Honestly look at and in yourself from top to bottom, left to right and front to back, daily."
—*Dalai Lama*

2. REORGANIZE: once you are able to recognize exactly what areas you need help in, your second growth and improvement prerequisite is to be able to reorganize your thoughts and habits accordingly.

In sports, one has to apply a tactic called mental rehearsal. Mental rehearsal is repetitively seeing yourself doing the new task in your mind. Imagine how you will breathe, what you'll say, how you'll say it, your body posture, hand gestures, your facial expressions; practice doing those perfectly in your imagination. Picture it clearly, to the point where you actually feel it is happening.

The emotional (limbic) and habitual (amygdala) parts of your brain can't actually tell the difference between what is real and what is imagined (neocortex), so really get engaged in those mental rehearsals. This will cause new neural pathways to fire together and then wire together! Then, when you go out into the real world to actually do it, it feels much more natural, and you are better prepared emotionally, physically and psychologically. When you stack mental rehearsal with practicing, drilling and rehearsing your sales techniques (out loud and with a great delivery), there is no end to how much you can improve!

When you start applying some of the concepts I have given you here, you will be changing both the surface and deep structure of your self-image. The more you repeat this, the more you will feel and behave like a skilled salesperson who is truly committed to his/her industry.

We know that repetition is the mother of skill. New and better results will follow almost immediately after you engage your brain regularly in playing out better selling situations and skills.

Duane Brain Tip

Reader, one of the most effective and time-honored ways to program change in yourself is to lock onto a mental image of whom and what you want to be, and then say with true feeling, "I am THAT I am!" over and over. I have used this to improve my golf score, relationships with my kids, my health habits and almost everything else!

The best time to sell something is right after you've made a sale—or right after you've imagined a sale. Over one hundred years of scientific research shows that our intention, emotions and thoughts do indeed affect the probability of our end results, so be very mindful of what you allow your dominant thoughts to be.

You may want to search on Google and YouTube for Dr.

Emoto, Kirlain Photography, and Quantum Physics. And buckle up, because it may change your understanding of everything, including how you can improve your life and sales.

3. HABITUATE: the third growth and improvement prerequisite is that you have to execute your new successful activities daily. You need to be obsessive about it and take massive action so that you start getting better results, develop some positive momentum, and really ingrain those new behaviors and habits into your daily routine.

Duane Brain Tip

Reader, some selling situations do not come up very often, so, after you master something such as how to overcome an uncommon objection, be sure to review your notes on it periodically. You need to make sure it stays in your accessible decision-making mind space, thereby allowing you to remember it when you need it again!

Two Common Deadly Traits

There are two traits that I'm going to warn you of that are very detrimental for any individual, company or country: arrogance and ignorance. When somebody embodies either trait, it's bad. If they embody both simultaneously, it's a disaster waiting to happen.

Arrogance and ignorance are lethal when it comes to the success of businesses and individuals. Don't confuse arrogance with confidence. Be confident but humble! Being sure of yourself is a wonderful thing, but know that there is always more to learn.

Avoid individuals who are arrogant or ignorant, and make sure you are not that way. With those types of personalities, people often don't understand where they need help and often think they're above needing help. Cocky and complacent types think they can walk on water and that their stuff doesn't stink, and they often take it all for granted. Entire corporations and countries are guilty of this, and it is a major predictor of impending failure.

If you have that attitude, you're going to risk losing it all.

Your Environment and Personal Spaces

People surround themselves with things they like, are interested in or are comfortable with. During a sale, this offers you, the salesperson, an opportunity to profile and rapidly connect with them at their vehicle or when they are talking about themselves.

Just think of what I could find out about you if I were to scan over your bookshelves, your trunk, hear what music you've listened to, or see what is currently on your TV. I would learn quite a bit.

I attended a series of body language workshops several years ago along with some customs and police officers, and I found out how much people reveal about themselves via their personal patterns.

Imagine if you had somebody's IP address, and you could pick up what they look at on Google or YouTube, what their favorites are, their history of websites they've been to, and even where they have spent their time and their money. What would those patterns tell you about someone? Almost everything! What do those patterns say about you and what you are interested in? If I investigated your patterns, would I find any evidence that you were trying to improve your sales or income?

Your Career Can Be Easy or Difficult

If you have a hobby—whatever it may be—you do it because you enjoy it. It doesn't feel like work. Maybe you even go out of your way to watch shows and read magazines about it. You'll spend hours on it because you love it. If you could study this career—this profession, this trade that you're involved in—in the way that you study your hobby, chances are you'll find something about it that you love, and great success will find you.

What about your sales career can you fall in love with besides the money? Maybe you like helping people. Maybe you like the freedom of making the amount of money you want. Maybe you like that you can develop so many different skills about your language and body language and refine how you deal with people, and that these skills are transferable to your personal life. Perhaps you like the idea that eventually you can create your own hours by working through appointments; or perhaps you like that it is a mental challenge for you to learn new sales skills, product knowledge, and how different cultures buy and trade. Maybe you like that you can make more money than you need so that you can help someone in your family or your favorite charity. Maybe you like it because it might allow you to retire earlier, or maybe it is going to be something that you don't need to retire from because you never really want to retire.

I get a huge level of fulfillment from all these benefits of being in sales and sales training, and it makes my trade a painless passion. I can also tell you firsthand how much more you will love your career if you absolutely own and master some major skills. It's fun to be good!

Stop hoping for things to be easier, and start working on you getting better!

—*Jim Rohn*

Duane Brain Tip

Reader, in sales, you are essentially self-employed, so make the decision now to walk out of your career and not be carried out. Sooner or later, you may want to or have to stop working. If you are smart with your money, that will be a viable option. But so often, I find great people in sales with a lot of life left at the end of their money. Jokingly, maybe they planned on dying early, and that just didn't happen. It really becomes more about what you *do* with the money you make than about how much money you make.

The only difference between work and play comes down to whether or not you like what you're doing. One of the greatest things about the business we're in is that it can fulfill so many different needs. It gives you a lot of security, variety, significance, contribution, growth, and connections with people. It allows you to do these things at a high level, which is great because once your financial needs are satisfied, you might not be driven to your next level just by money. As with anything that you really want or are really interested in, I believe you can and should study it effortlessly, just like a hobby.

The shortcut to success involves the knowledge of what to do, a passion for what you do, ever-increasing confidence and skills, and a sense of doing something worthwhile for others. When you do what you love and are good at it, time disappears, and you won't even feel like your career is *work*!

CHAPTER 5

Understanding Our Industry: Statistics vs. Trends

In many lines of business, statistics are used to compare or target production for the future. This can be a very useful tool. However, in sales, they can be used very differently. As mentioned earlier, I avoid soft sales statistics for a very good reason. Any sales statistics you see such as "89% of salespeople do this," or "71% of buyers do that" are questionable.

In car sales in particular, the questions I ask when I see those statistics are, "When and where (in what country, state or province) was that statistic compiled, and was it based on new or used cars, and on what brand?"

Not only do numbers like that change over time, but they have changed drastically in the last ten years due to the Internet and other major changes in buyer expectations and behavior. They are also extremely regional, being driven by things like the dominant cultures in the area.

Statistics generated and tracked by your place of business and your own store's traffic are valid because they are your own specifically. This is why I would caution you against building a business plan around "industry statistics" that someone else put together, often with data that can't be validated or data that is entirely fabricated. It doesn't pass the sniff test if they aren't willing to send you the actual data and surveys.

It's not uncommon for training companies to throw around exact percentages so they can appear like research houses in order to give their material more credibility and buy-in. Be careful how much weight you put on those numbers.

It isn't uncommon for a company to add unnecessary complexities to their numbers. They might run a bunch of numbers and then advise you to "take this number times that number, add it to this number, divide it by that number, and multiply it over here. You are selling this amount right now, but you should be selling that amount based on these numbers."

This is a cheap selling tactic on their part, done in a way to beat up salespeople and thereby exaggerate the need for their training and development services. It's meant to make people believe that they need to continue with the training program they sell, since the statistics they use always make everyone look like useless under-performers.

Then they'll tell you something like, "Now, take that number, and take a quarter of this number (or half of that number), and let's chop it into eighths six times, and—voila!—you should still be selling a lot more than you are!"

I have a big problem with that because it is all built on false premises and downright arbitrary numbers. Any institution, business, or agency that uses complicated formulas to manipulate soft data into results of their own choosing very likely has a hidden agenda of their own.

When it comes to soft numbers or trends, I try to use words like "most", "some", "many", and "few", which are words that indicate trends, to differentiate them from hard data.

Remember that the trend is your friend. If you understand

that and operate alongside it, there is nothing you won't be able to adapt to.

Below are fifteen trends I would like you to read. When you read them, just check in quickly with your head, heart and gut and then tick off if you think it is true or false for your marketplace and brand today. There is no wrong or right, good or bad, true or false. In reality, it is about your awareness of your industry as of right now.

After you do that, we'll take up the seven most important of these trends in greater detail in the next chapter. Have fun!

Remember that <u>the trend is your friend</u>. If you understand that and operate alongside it, there is nothing you won't be able to adapt to.

FIFTEEN TRENDS

1. There are dozens of brands, hundreds of models and almost infinite choices for used vehicles.

— It's getting more difficult to have constant price or product advantages.

❏ True ❏ False

2. Most buyers use the Internet to research price and product information.

— Your prospective buyers sometimes know more (or think they do) about the product than you.

❏ True ❏ False

3. Some of a buyer's product knowledge and money questions are actually credibility tests.

— Product knowledge and price can be dangerous territories with some customers.

❏ True ❏ False

4. Very few people actually buy vehicles online, and most online purchases are long-distance used vehicle transactions.

—The Internet gives us access to new markets.

❏ True ❏ False

5. Many people buy something different than they originally requested.

— We're not order takers, as they often don't buy the exact product researched.

❏ True ❏ False

6. Many people buy because they connected with the salesperson on some level.

— Unlike the products you sell, you are not available anywhere else.

❑ True ❑ False

7. There has been a major decline in the number of daily walk-ins in the past ten to fifteen years.

— Buyers don't need to go from store to store to get basic information.

❑ True ❑ False

8. Three or four walk-ins per day per rep used to be the industry average, now maybe one or two is average.

— One buyer might shop us two to three times using just the Internet and phone.

❑ True ❑ False

9. About 100 units per year is what most salespeople have always delivered.

— The average volume per salesperson has been fairly consistent over time.

❑ True ❑ False

10. Twenty to twenty-five walk-ins per month per rep is average, and this yields about five or six sales.

— We have no control over how many people may walk in.

❑ True ❑ False

11. Six to eight appointments per month per rep is the industry average, yielding three or four more sales.

— We have some control over how many appointments we can create.

❏ True ❏ False

12. Low first-visit closing ratio vs. high-appointment closing ratio.

— Appointments from any source generally buy more often than walk-ins.

❏ True ❏ False

13. Most of our customers can't remember our names after one year.

— People can't send me more business if they can't remember me.

❏ True ❏ False

14. Most salespeople spend most of their shifts waiting for walk-ins.

— We may have a few minutes a day when we could be more productive.

❏ True ❏ False

15. Most people have an email address and cell phone, and they message using texting, Facebook, LinkedIn, Twitter, etc.

— We could ask for email addresses, cell phone numbers, text numbers, and social media profiles, and use these more.

❏ True ❏ False

CHAPTER 6

Relevant Industry Trends

In this chapter, we will have a closer look at some of the trends identified in the last chapter. All of the trends are valuable, but there are a few that should be elaborated on. (The trends are discussed as they are positioned in the list in the previous chapter.)

By the way, when you read through the trends, did you find that most were true for your area or dealership? In fact, most are true in almost all markets today, and I have recently used them at workshops as far apart as Halifax and Honolulu!

Most buyers use the Internet to research price and product information.

—Your prospective buyers sometimes know more (or think they do) about the product than you.

Who knows or cares if it is 89%, 76%, or 51%? What matters is that the majority of customers these days do their research online. Because of the massive choices to be found online, the hardest part of the sale is already over by the time they actually contact you or walk in, as the Internet could have sent them anywhere. That's the real takeaway here.

Did you check off true or false? I'm willing to guess, if you're in sales today, you checked off "True" because it happens to be true in every market I have sold or trained in recently, and I've been in most.

That relates to the next statement, which says:

Some of a buyer's product knowledge and money questions are credibility tests.

—Product knowledge and price can be dangerous territories with some customers.

Is that true or false? I believe it's very true.

If you give the EXACT price, payment, availability or specifications on your feet in the store, to an email lead or a sales call, then you may create a couple of problems. It's hard to establish an absolute rule here, but once you've given a price, payment or specification, you've really committed yourself to it. Even if you're just a little bit off, this could hurt you later on in the sale. If the buyer has obtained other information from the Internet (which isn't always accurate) or from another company or brand (which aren't always correct or honest), which they believe is more valid or favorable than what you've told them, you lose either credibility or connection with them. What's worse is they might not even bother telling you as they proceed through the sales process with you.

A buyer might ask you, "Hey, what's the price? What's the program? What's the rate? What's the availability? What are the specifications?" When you commit yourself to answering those questions too specifically, you run a great risk of losing credibility and/or connection with this buyer on the spot. If what you tell them conflicts with what they expect to hear, they might not believe you, like you, trust you or respect you no matter what you say after that.

There is a B.G. (Before Google) old-school saying in the business that states, "Stay off price." These days, you shouldn't stay off price entirely; just stay off EXACT price.

I strongly suggest that you get very comfortable giving people accurate but loose rounded price ranges—round numbers, or "rubber payments" as I call them, that are non-specific and non-committal. And when they want more detail, you can tell them, "That's a great question. There are a lot of variables, and things change all the time, so, as long as we're in the right ballpark, let's just iron out the specifics back at my workstation or when you come in."

You don't want to stay off price entirely, and you don't want to get into an exact price too soon. By mastering an ineffective and outdated technique, such as, "Stay off price," a few unwanted things can happen. First of all, you have just created a major distraction for your customer. Their unanswered question will hang around like the proverbial elephant in the room, and their attention will get stuck on what you won't talk about.

If the buyer pointedly asks you what the monthly cost might be or what they are looking at price-wise, and you brush it off with comments like, "Don't worry about it, we'll discuss it later," or, "It doesn't matter, we'll handle it." My friends, to the buyer, it *does* matter. Do you think they are stupid? They won't forget that question, and, to them, it is an important one. If you refuse to address it at all, you will start to look a little suspicious as if you have something to hide. They might think that you are incompetent or perhaps even untrustworthy. Why would someone train you to use a dishonest technique?

Avoiding price, their unanswered question will hang around like the proverbial elephant in the room, and their attention will get stuck on what you won't talk about.

If they ask you a second or third time, and you continue to dodge the question by changing the topic, you could really lose traction and credibility in their eyes. Your refusal to address their question at all could seriously impair your ability to create any level of rapport or connection with the buyer. They may think you're staying off price because you don't know your prices, which ruins your credibility. Most people don't want to deal with a salesperson who demonstrates that they don't know their trade.

What if the customer had already been online to get information, as almost all have? They know what the price is, and yet you, the sales professional, won't discuss it. These people can become awfully frustrated because now they are actually in front of a salesperson who works for the company but can't get any clarification. Not to mention the fact that you may have spent one or two hours with them, studiously avoiding price, only to find out that they don't qualify or the price is too high. You can end up wasting valuable time as you may be on the wrong product entirely. This happens daily with salespeople who are professional price avoiders. In frustration, some people will even pull out their smartphone and wave it at you, asking you if the information they found out on their own is correct or not!

There is something in sales training called the price value formula. The price value formula clearly states that "When the value exceeds the price, the customer will buy." Notice there is a relationship between those two. By definition, a relationship involves two things; in this case, they are: value and price. So guess what, Sparky, if the customer has no idea what the price is, it is impossible to build value because there is nothing for them to compare and relate it to.

By learning how to "stay off EXACT price" and discuss rounded-off price and payment ranges, you will save time, create FLOW, allow yourself and your buyer to work through important preliminary price ranges and product benefits—simultaneously qualifying people on the product—and you'll build real relative value and credibility. Last but not least, you will get that elephant out of the room so they can actually listen to the rest of your presentation.

Once a buyer gives you the green light on the payment and price ranges, their full attention can be put into appreciating and understanding you and the product. After given a price range, some buyers will follow up with specific questions that you may want to answer now or later. In order to maintain your FLOW, respond to specific price-related questions in a manner such as, "Mr./Mrs. Buyer, that's a great question. I'm quite certain we will be between X and Y. Anything I can't read on the product, we will verify back at my workstation." (Say this while gesturing to your workstation, smiling and nodding.)

That type of response makes you look knowledgeable, credible, caring, and meticulous enough to not make a mistake on something that may be important to your buyer. It also helps us maintain FLOW, save time and deflect small, irrelevant questions.

Any question that was not brought up again later was either indirectly addressed by you along the way or not really that important to them. If you lose any traction by ignoring important questions or giving specific or unacceptable information, your buyer may not trust or believe you later on when it comes to deciding if they should buy and pay for it.

Duane Brain Tip

Reader, much like price, you may want to stay away from EXACT specifications during the sale, and just keep the sale moving forward based on ranges and getting those details back at your desk. If the price or specification range isn't in the right ballpark for what your buyer wants or needs, give them alternatives, and make suggestions and adjustments to what you are selling them until everything starts coming together! Such as, "Would you consider a smaller model but up the package with a longer term, different features, different finance terms or more money down?"

People like to make choices, so explain to them what their options are and why you are suggesting them. If you are in the wrong range, then the exact figures are not relevant.

Beyond prices and specs, there are availability questions such as, "How soon can I have it?"

This type of question is a buying signal, so you would naturally respond with a statement such as, "How soon would you want it?" And if they respond with a time frame or date, you counter with a soft trap. "If we could get it ready by then, would it go into your name, or someone else's?" If that came in favorably, you then would softly trap further with, "Let's double check availability and delivery times back at my workstation. And we can also wrap up any other small details that are important to you, okay?"

Don't just jump in and answer with things like, "We can get it right away," or, "We can't get it." Don't disappoint yourself or your customers with EXACT availability, prices or specifications; and don't give open-ended, non-trapping answers like, "Maybe in a couple of days, hours, or weeks." Failure to cash in on a valuable buying signal can cost you the sale as another signal may not present itself again later. To summarize, here's the tag line for this one:

"Beware of exact pricing, payments, specifications, or availability on your feet; these are always handled better in your seat."

As said repeatedly, you do want to give people some sort of an idea, as you don't want to avoid their questions entirely. Remember to give ranges, round numbers and rubber payments on the phone, to email leads and lot traffic, and handle the exact details at your workstation whenever possible. Stop trying to master an outdated B.G., and now harmful, technique such as "Stay off price!"

Many people buy because they connect with the salesperson on some level.

—Unlike the products you sell, you are not available anywhere else.

That's true.

The uniqueness of you, your own brilliance, personality, quirkiness, and your individuality is unique and should be leveraged. It's also a big part of your company's success. All your new products are available anywhere for about the same price, and they were probably even built in the same factory. So what you are really selling is yourself! And, of course, your pre-owned products are unique and one of a kind, just like you! So study them as individuals, and sell the fact that they are priced accordingly. Show off their strong points, personality traits and blemishes!

There has been a major decline in the number of daily walk-ins in the past ten to fifteen years.

—Buyers don't need to go from store to store to get basic information.

This is true.

I've been in the business long enough to remember what it was like when I was a "lot boy" on Saturdays. Back in the '80s and '90s, every Saturday was mayhem because that was the day when most people were off work and the day when dealerships were open. It's hard to imagine, but back then, people still had to physically go in to see what was sitting on the lot and to get price and product information.

Nowadays, people can find out about your inventory or pricing from the comfort of their own homes and smartphones, so now they are more like destination shoppers. By the time they contact us, they are looking to see where they can buy, rather than what to buy. What has happened, then, is that the Internet has become the most tremendous value-building setup tool we could ever ask for. We are getting more phone and email traffic and less walk-in traffic, and the people who contact us are a lot closer to making a decision and are much more transaction ready than they ever were.

I'll assert that, as of the time of writing this book, well more than half of your traffic expects to buy the product on their first visit, and if they don't, they are disappointed. In other words, by the time they walk in, they are totally or almost sold, and, if you don't make any mistakes, the sale is yours.

Duane Brain Tip

Reader, like staying off price, we used to be told to "Slow Them Down!" I have a serious warning for you: all of our attention spans are lowering every year, so as soon as your customers feel as though they are being slowed down, or when you leave them alone, they get agitated or bored, and they may start scheming against you while they pull out their smartphones.

Every time they go on their smartphones or are given the time to mentally drift off, your control and profit drop. You have to learn to keep things FLOWing or you will pay the price in terms of lost sales, lower profits and eroded customer satisfaction.

The remainder of your traffic still needs to be sold. They need to know the features, advantages and benefits of the product more extensively. They require a longer sales process because they are really not sure what they are buying and are likely comparing your brand against another's.

Your ability to understand your individual buyer's psychology and to not skip the most important steps for that buyer (but also not drag it out and talk yourself out of a sale) is fundamental to your success today. This will be one of your six "sales powers", which we will take up very soon.

Most of our customers can't remember our names after one year.

—People can't send you more business if they can't remember you.

Do you recall that, earlier, I asked you to write down the names of any salespeople you could remember who had sold you anything? Did you remember anyone? If you did, those individuals were memorable and proved valuable after the sale and cared about you as more than just someone with money in his or her wallet. As a result, you remembered them and probably sent them a referral or two or bought from them again.

Later on in this book, I'll present a formula that I've unpacked from the most successful salespeople I've ever met. It will help you become favorably memorable and become their first point of association regarding the products you sell. That means that the buyer will associate you with the product, and you will be the one they call in regard to the product they bought; whether it needs repair, they need another one, or their friend also needs something similar. This way, you can set yourself apart from your competition and get all the calls. Help your customers out no matter why they call, and you'll also get all of the referrals and repeat business from those clients.

Most salespeople spend most of their shifts waiting for walk-ins.

—We may have a few minutes a day when we could be more productive.

Most showrooms and store fronts will tell you that this is true; although, it's not so true for your angels. Angels are people who do not rely on the front door for their business, and they do not stand around trying to sell cars to each other all day. Instead, they have created their own network through texting, Facebook, LinkedIn, being memorable and valuable after the sale, emails, taking/making phone calls, and extreme customer service.

Angels aside, for most salespeople, yes, there are absolutely a few more minutes a day where they can be more productive. In fact, your power of time management will be one of your sales powers.

As I'm sure you know, the best salespeople spend the most time in their offices, and the best sales managers spend the most time on the sales floor!

Most people have an email address and cell phone, and they message using texting, Facebook, LinkedIn, Twitter, etc.

—We could ask for email addresses, cell phone numbers, text numbers, and social media profiles, and use these more.

This is very true for most markets I am in.

Just think about social media and your ability right now to connect with so many people and find transaction ready consumers. Remember my law of 2500 that I mentioned earlier?

To conclude this chapter, here are some quick stories to illustrate what I have been talking about as well as a few additional tips.

About a year ago, I was on our car lot trying to sell a vehicle to an individual who had originated as an email lead. From his emailed questions, we took it to the phone and then to text messaging. We confirmed an appointment, and I could tell he knew a lot about this particular product. He even knew about the lineage of the car manufacturer, which was actually a pretty interesting conversation.

He showed up right on time at 4:10 p.m., and it was nice to see this as it was an odd time. I walked across the street to show him the vehicle, and I really had to make a decision in terms of how I would show him that car. I didn't want to jeopardize my credibility and connection that had been built—especially with a customer who knew so much more about the brand and vehicle than I did. So I made the decision to simply hand him the keys and say, "Mr. Buyer, I can tell you know a lot about the vehicle, the manufacturer and everything else, so here are the keys to the vehicle. I'd be honored if you'd walk me around it, and if there's anything else you'd like me to find out, I'd be happy to get that for you."

He really liked that. He smiled, laughed and said, "I really appreciate that," as he knew he was a real hobbyist and aficionado of this particular brand.

He said, "For now, I don't need the keys. Just pop the locks if you could."

I hit the key fob and opened the doors for him. He asked me if the central control on the computer that sits by the dash and gear shift was working. I told him, "Absolutely, and here are the keys if you want to try it."

He said, "Oh, no, no, no. I don't need that on this particular vehicle. With this make and year, you just push these two buttons and hold them down for two seconds simultaneously, and the computer will fire up along with the stereo and the entire electrical system."

My jaw dropped. I'd never seen anything like it. I laughed and said, "Man, am I ever glad I didn't try to take you around the car." He just chuckled and kept going.

This is the level of knowledge some people have nowadays on vehicles. They can get it online or from friends or technicians. And sometimes you just have to get out of the way and let people sell themselves. This is not just for cars; it's the same with other products as well.

Duane Brain Tip

Reader, start your product presentations at the simplest positions, such as the trunk. Use that position as a place to warm up to each other and find out about simple usage, needs, and wants.

As you approach the more complex technical positions, such as under the hood, say something like, "I'm not a technician, but how important are the details to you, and do you have any specific questions?" This will ensure you win over everyone and that you never get yourself into a bind during a presentation with today's diverse buyers. And of course, anything you can't read on the product can be specifically addressed at your desk!

Major warning with today's buyers: if you give and commit to specific product information, you run the very high risk of losing credibility on the details that don't match what they read online, or give an otherwise transaction ready buyer the sudden realization that perhaps they have not done enough research. In simple terms, you may un-sell someone who came in sold!

Here's another quick story:

I had a couple come in to look at an upscale, white car we had in inventory—something a little bit older but still a very nice vehicle in great condition.

They pulled into the lot with a white vehicle as well, but of another upscale brand and also a lot newer.

On this particular day, I dropped by the lot in shorts, a t-shirt, and sandals. It was a hot August afternoon, and I had planned on reconciling the inventory—making sure the physical inventory matched the virtual inventory we had posted online. I thought I'd only be there for an hour or so.

Our used car operation is fairly small, but even so, you can't go in for just an hour. Most of our business is service, and we're also surrounded by a bunch of income properties we own. We'd have to completely change our entire property-focused business model to be able to stock and sell a lot more used cars.

As the couple drove up and I went outside to greet them, I laughed to myself, thinking, *This is not going to go very well*, because I didn't look professional to say the least.

I walked over to this couple who were in their fifties and very well-dressed, and the wife smiled at me and said, "Good morning!" She was very talkative, but her husband wouldn't even acknowledge me. He actually rolled his eyes and looked away when he first saw me, and I knew it was because of how I looked. Remember, most people judge a book by it's cover.

After a few minutes around the car, he still hadn't responded or engaged with me at all. I had to make a decision and finally decided to use a bit of reverse psychology. Since it was clear he wasn't going to talk to me, and because I was very hot, I was getting a little irritated and really just wanted to go inside where it was air-conditioned, and I could get done the things I came in to do. Wrong attitude, perhaps, but that's how I felt. I said to the couple, "Well, I don't want to bother you. I can see you want your own space here, and I can also see you've done your research."

This was not a random guess; he had parked his car and walked over in such a way that I knew what he was looking for, and with print-outs under his arm, it was obvious he had done his research without even talking to him. I told the couple, "What I'll do here is leave you alone. I'll be inside. All the cars are locked up. Now, if you want more details about a vehicle, I can bring the keys out to you. But I can tell you this: there are about a half-dozen things about this car that aren't so great that are going to take you some time to discover. But I don't want to bother you, so enjoy looking over the car."

As soon as I said that, he turned to me and said, "What? Excuse me. What was that?"

"There are a few things about the car that are a bit hard to find; every pre-owned vehicle is unique," I explained. "I know the car really well because we've been servicing it pretty much since it was new, but I don't want to bother you."

He said, "Well, what are they?"

"Great question. Let's go get the keys." And NOT "Wait here while I get the keys." You must strive to maintain FLOW and keep your customer with you and engaged at all times so they don't start scheming against you.

Duane Brain Tip

Reader, I try to bring the customer with me everywhere I go so that they aren't left alone becoming agitated, bored, and back on their smartphones. When I have to leave a customer alone when closing the sale, I will play a product video if I think they aren't sold on the car or a cute comedy video to keep them occupied and entertained. More FLOW means more dough. Today, its all about the customer experience.

Sometimes, with certain buyers, if they're analytical, assertive, a little arrogant or aggressive, the last thing they want to hear is some salesperson try to "sell them the car," especially one they think they already know everything about.

We all chatted together on the walk to get the keys. "So, what do you do during the day when you aren't shopping for cars!?"

We brought the keys and a dealer plate out, and I started to go around the car. I showed him a few unique little personality traits and blemishes that all used cars have—a minor scratch on the rim, a missing cigarette lighter, and I also pointed out the odometer, which was pretty high for the year.

At the odometer, I said, "You know this already because you've been to our website. I can see that."

He said, "Absolutely."

As I went around the car, I actually had to go out of my way to back up my earlier statement of, "There are some things not so great about this car," because, in truth, it was a gem. Standing at the back of the car, I opened the trunk and said, "Some people have told me that the trunk is too big."

He asked, "What do you mean?"

"It's a little too big for some people."

He laughed and said, "Well, that's why I want it, because my car is a little too small. We do a lot of golfing."

On almost every personality trait or blemish that I pointed out, I gained a little more credibility because I wasn't hiding anything. Of course, I also gave him rubber payments.

On virtually all points, he said, "Well, that's not a big deal," or, "I expected that," and, "Yes, you already disclosed that online." All of these only increased my credibility and connection.

Here's the line to remember from this story: sometimes disclosing what is not great is great. One of the first questions used car buyers ask these days is, "Do you have the police, accident and insurance report on this car?" The reason is that when the customer goes online to do their search, up come all the vehicles that match their basic parameters. They can sift through cars that have too many miles or kilometers, cars that are the wrong color, wrong features, and dealerships that clearly don't disclose things properly.

Of course, it's all priced accordingly, and price is one of the easiest online sorting criteria. It's the same with any product someone wants to buy. Then they end up with their hot list. The hot list will usually be three to five cars or products that they will call about, email, or go in person to see.

Therefore, one of the most popular questions people have on the used car lot is, "What's wrong with the car?" If you sell any used item, it would be the same sort of question. The reason they ask this is because the vehicle already seems to meet all the other positive criteria they found out when researching on their own online, or else they wouldn't be there! If you then avoid personality traits and blemishes, or if you don't know how to bring them up during your walk around, demo drive, or pricing segment, it can hurt your sales. With a good majority of today's buyers coming in transaction ready, thanks to the Internet, they have a totally different set of questions than they had 10 or more years ago—B.G.

EXERCISE

Before we leave this chapter and move to the next, I would like you to search on Google and YouTube for a few items. The first thing is, "How do I buy a car?" Watch a few videos, and read some of the information that's available online. You'll see things such as sales trainers in the automotive industry telling salespeople to do some not-so-ethical things to consumers.

That's irresponsible. As a trainer, I would never put anything on the Internet that I wouldn't want my or your customers to see.

You're also going to see a lot of crazy information on what the customer should or shouldn't do when they come in.

At the time of the writing of this book, if you Google, "How do I buy a car?" the basic trends that come up in almost every article are:

— Never buy on the first visit.

— Drive the car, get pricing and then leave. Make your decision a few days later when you are not quite as excited, and never drive the car the same day you make a buying decision.

— Ask for their best price, and if they won't talk price, walk out.

— Make excuses why you can't buy that day. Examples: your wife isn't there, you haven't shopped for insurance yet, wallet is at home, etc.

— When you do phone or email around, phone or email the same dealership and talk to three or four different salespeople so you can double-check the information inside the building. Do not deal with the sales rep more than once or twice online or on the phone, and don't deal with the same salesperson when you come in.

— Make sure you tell them you do not have a trade (until after pricing on their new car is ironed out), and don't act like you like them or their car too much because you'll be taken advantage of.

That is the kind of advice available on the Internet for car buyers. The same can exist for any product that you sell. By just understanding those trends, and particularly after reading about the sales powers and the use of verbal and body language later in this book, you will see why you may want to consider making some changes to the way you sell if you're still running a B.G. sales process.

Many of your customers are talking about, hearing, or reading online about how to deal with different salespeople. Another useful thing you should do is search on Google and YouTube for your product and search out the pros and cons, advantages and disadvantages that people are posting about it.

With some buyer profiles, knowing the so-called cons of your inventory may gain you a lot of traction in the sale. When you know ahead of time what your buyer might criticize, you can be prepared to handle it. You can even move with confidence in the direction of the objection—i.e., bring up some concerns that will probably surface later —earlier in the sale, when you want to. That way, it can't be used against you later in the sale when you least expect it.

One thing to know is that the only reason some product critics and consumer advocates even have a job is because they point out things that are not so wonderful—or often even true—about cars, trucks, vans and SUVs.

The same could be said for other products, but the car

business is a common target of ridicule. And once critics start to read each others' articles, negative press can start to catch on like wildfire. Other advocates and critics start pointing out the same as they write about trends on the Internet and build their own version of "credibility" for their audiences.

The Internet is a massive forum and storehouse for complaints. There are very few people who post, "Oh I love this place/product! You're wonderful!" And because people are drawn to complaints and buyer-beware warnings, others will write them, whether real or fake, to their own benefit. Unfortunately, many individuals tend to listen to it all because they're afraid of being taken advantage of.

Knowing What's in Your Inventory

There is a saying in the car business that goes back almost a hundred years and is still valid: "Walk the lot." What it means is, just like a person working in a grocery store, you have to know what's on the shelves and what's coming and going.

These days, however, walking the lot is not enough because your customers usually surf your lot on the Internet before they physically walk it. Some customers will even surf it with their smartphones or tablets *while* they walk it. You don't want to lose any credibility or connection by not knowing your virtual inventory as well as your physical inventory. It becomes very difficult to take sales calls well or handle Internet leads if you don't know and understand your own virtual inventory. How many sales a year do you lose because you don't know your inventory or your website well enough?

So here's your new modern mantra: walk *and* surf your

lot—daily! Give management a daily hand to make sure the virtual inventory matches the physical inventory, because, if it doesn't, you will lose credibility and connection with your customers. Discrepancies come off as unprofessional and show that you don't really care or are disinterested in what you do. Who wants to put their trust in a disinterested amateur? No one. You never want the customer to think, *Am I talking to the wrong salesperson?!*

If you ask your sales calls, "Can you please tell me the stock number of the item that you're looking at right now online?" most will tell you, because with the majority of your sales calls, people are on their computer or smartphones while they phone you.

With that in mind, you MUST know your physical inventory, and you have to know what your website says about your own product.

This has been a summary of just a few good ideas and common-sense tips. After having read the above trends, I hope you have identified a few things that you could do better, things that you're already doing, and things that you can start to do.

Now that we have set up some basic sales concepts, we will start to cover your six sales powers in detail.

.

CHAPTER 7

The Six Sales Powers

Codifying Success and Modeling

I found myself in a unique position. I have been formally educated in many areas of sales, psychology, and body language and hold several certifications in those areas (I continue to study them, and am just returning from workshops in Spain and Germany as I write this chapter.) These trainings and many others taught me how to model excellence by mapping out a person's internal world and observing their external processes and behaviors. When I found myself spending time with so many outstanding sales people over the past few years, I intentionally tried to unpack the differences that made the difference for them!

Again, what you do in modeling is you find somebody who is getting the results that you want, and then you investigate what they are doing that gets them those results. Then you make sure that in your own process you model their most effective habits and those crucial tendencies that make them successful.

This is not a random selection of stuff they do. You have to select the elements that are crucial to their success, but how do you know which ones are crucial? How do you weed them out from all the other things that they do? There is no secret intuition to use on this. You have to list them out and then check them out, one by one. Once you add all of these traits and skills together, you then start to eliminate them one at a time, noticing when your results start to suffer. If results suffer the moment that you weaken or remove a particular skill, habit or attitude, you know that that piece is crucial. It's a non-negotiable, essential item of the recipe. What you are left with is a highly efficient and effective map of success that anyone can follow to improve their own sales.

Remember my pasta sauce analogy earlier, about removing all the ingredients one by one, but the moment I take out the tomatoes, it's no longer a tomato sauce? Sure, the other ingredients are all important, but the tomatoes are the crucial ingredient. So what are a top salesperson's "tomatoes"?

Your "Tomatoes"—the Six Sales Powers

Over the course of several years, over many conversations, emails, phone calls and meetings with some really great salespeople, I would pay special attention to their visions, beliefs, attitudes and strategies—I tried to codify them to figure out what made them so successful. In the end, I came up with six fundamental traits, or "Six Sales Powers" as I call them, that are as crucial to your recipe for sales success or business success as tomatoes are to tomato sauce.

You might ask, how do I know that these six powers or traits are crucial? It's very simple: if you take out any one of these six things COMPLETELY, it becomes nearly impossible for you to sell anything to anyone! However, if you increase the levels of these six things to an extreme, you will have the formula for a highly successful salesperson, guaranteed!

What are these six sales powers? I will list them here and then go through them one by one, briefly discussing their importance. Then, in the following chapters, we will take each one up in much greater detail.

One thing that might be very useful to you is to assess yourself from one to ten in your own understanding and application of these six areas. A score of one would be not doing well in this area, and ten would be doing very well. Be honest with yourself when you do this so that you can see which areas you most need to improve in order to be more successful.

Rate yourself as these points seem to you now, and, later in the book, I will ask you to rate yourself again. This is because, at this point, you can only see yourself in the light of what you know now about these areas. You don't know what you don't know. My ways of explaining, viewing and looking at these six areas are quite unique, so, by the time you've read the book, you may see a change in how you view yourself entirely. For now, I will provide you with a brief overview of these six sales powers for you to familiarize yourself with.

1—Your Power of Customer Service

The first sales power is customer service. You probably think we're in sales, but really, we're in the customer service business. By servicing the customer, you are helping her buy *and* own something that she really needs and will use. The higher the level of customer service you bring to your customers and the more that you realize that the things you do are done *for* your customer and not *to* your customer, the more successful you are going to be, not only now, but also in obtaining crucial repeat and referral business in the future.

How do you rate in the customer service area? Do you sell and service your customers with everything you have, especially after the sale? Customer service is a crucial sales power.

RATE YOURSELF OUT OF 10 NOW: __/10

You probably think we're in sales, but really, we're in the customer service business.

2—Your Power of Communication and Use of Sales Language

The next sales power is communication and sales language. What you say, how you say it and what words you use are important. Using modern and up-to-date language is much more effective than old, stale or negative words. Also, you should be able to adapt your language to that of your buyer so that she feels comfortable with what you say and can relate to you as well. Communication and language skills is a fundamental sales power.

RATE YOURSELF OUT OF 10 NOW: __/10

3—Your Power of Building Relationships

Building relationships is the third sales power. With no additional information about this power, using only common sense for now, ask yourself, "Do I have a sufficiently huge quantity of quality repeats, referrals and networks so that I don't have to rely on walk-ins?"

If you sell a lot of product every month to your own network without relying on the front door, then you are, by definition, an angel. The more you have of these relationships, in terms of both high quality and high quantity, the more they'll drive your business without you having to wait for a walk-in. If the front door was welded shut tomorrow, would you still be able to survive?

You can't become successful without maximizing your power of building excellent relationships.

RATE YOURSELF OUT OF 10 NOW: __/10

4—Your Power of Making Effective Use of Your Time

Your next sales power is effective time management. How would you rate yourself on this one? Base your rating on this premise: "I never waste time just waiting around hoping to sell something, and I don't spend my time talking with other salespeople during my money hours."

Like all other powers, if you waste your time to an extreme, your sales stop. So, time management is a tomato.

RATE YOURSELF OUT OF 10 NOW: __/10

5—Your Power of Body Language

There has been much said already about body language, and this is the next sales power. Would you say that you have mastered the art of effective communication using your hands, body, facial expressions and tone, and can read other people like a mind reader?

The better you are with body language, the more effective and efficient you will be in all your communications and interactions.

RATE YOURSELF OUT OF 10 NOW: __/10

6—Your Power of State of Mind and Focus

The last sales power is your state of mind and your ability to focus. Can you stay on track, be positive, and focus on your major and minor goals daily? We know the best time to sell something is right after you have sold something, and some days are better than others, but how often do you feel really focused and positive? State of mind and focus are what drive your ability to use all your other powers. It is perhaps the biggest tomato in the recipe.

RATE YOURSELF OUT OF 10 NOW: __/10

Now that you have been introduced to the Six Sales Powers (your "tomatoes", or what could be called crucial sales traits), we will take a look at each one more in-depth in the following chapters.

Here's the wonderful thing. Whatever your level of success is now, I know that to some degree you are already applying some of the good principles, practices, psychology, patterns, and probability that I spoke of in an earlier chapter, along with these six powers, or you wouldn't be in sales.

We will move forward, uncover and come to know these six different crucial areas, and I will show you how to vastly increase your power in all of them. As you move your power up in any one of these six areas, your sales will automatically improve. If you move your powers up significantly in all areas at the same time, you'll see dramatic changes as countless clients of mine have.

I receive countless emails from salespeople who have read my newsletters or attended my workshops, and who found that after putting these areas into motion, they began to sell a lot more product in a lot less time for a greater average dollar transaction per sale.

If you haven't done so already, based on what you know about these areas right now, please go back and rate your utilization of these six powers on a scale of one to ten. Then add your scores up, and divide that number by six. This will give you your average current potential out of ten. Save this rating and your understanding of these six areas, and see how it changes by the end of the book.

"Vitamin L"

Now that you have completed your self-assessment and

you have a better idea where you currently stand and what your potential is, we can move forward. There is one last point to touch on before we move on to the next chapter. What I have noticed is that everybody has what I call a "Vitamin L" deficiency. Vitamin L is the most important vitamin you need to survive. Vitamin L is Love. If you love your business, love your future, love yourself, love those in your life who are important to you, and love your customers as much as you should, you're going to do a much better job as a person and as a salesperson, and you will be reciprocated accordingly. Vitamin L makes more success obtainable and sustainable.

Let me frame the next few chapters by reminding you that all of your success in sales and the maximization of your sales powers comes down to your ability and willingness to build relationships. Your goal is to have people feel better about themselves after dealing and talking with you than they did before.

NOTE: All of the profit recovery and sales-building concepts in this book, as well as many other strategies, can be presented to a group of any size through our NAASSA training division. We can come directly to your company on-site or to your area for a regional event. And all are available online on MarinoTV, which has a library of almost 2000 videos to educate and motivate you.

We also have a call center and can be your BDC for hire, creating traffic and sales for you, working the phones and calling people in your market.

Contact us at 1-888-735-6275, email us at info@ duanemarino.com, or visit www.DuaneMarino.com for more information.

Chapter 8

Power #1: Your Power of Customer Service

Let's take a look at your first sales power in detail. This power is a big one, and it's called the Power of Customer Service to Build Relationships. Now, as previously mentioned, a great sales process is something you do *for* your customer, not something you do *to* your customer. Great customer service is not possible without loving what you do. Along with viewing yourself as a salesperson (rather than just as a person in sales), you also have to be able to apply what I call intention-based selling.

Your intentions behind your actions are crucial. Bad intentions cause negative consequences in direct and indirect ways. What is this thing I call "intention-based selling"? Intention is the reason you do something. When you sell something, you should intend to make money, intend to help someone buy something they need or want, and intend to service that person. Intention is an important commodity, and because people can sense your intentions, they will affect your career now and down the road. Positive intention should be a predominant theme throughout your sales day and selling activities. In addition, all your interactions with everyone around you, your coworkers and customers alike, should start and end with intelligent and good intentions.

"Begin with the end in mind."

—*Stephen Covey*

Earlier, I had mentioned that part of the end game was to give everyone a little "Vitamin L", and if your intentions are good, Vitamin L will be reciprocated along the way right back at you. I know it sounds a little corny, but I have found it to be very true. When you inject Vitamin L in everything you do, you're going to make better decisions and approach your tasks with a higher energy level. People are going to pick up on that. When you lead with love, good customer service is easy. Love your career or trade, love of making money for yourself and your family, love your brand and company, love your future, and love your customer. This will all translate into doing a better job, but this doesn't mean you have to actually *love* all your customers or that the customer is always right!

I have sold lots of things to people I don't like, even when the customer was wrong. People might buy from those they like, but they are more likely to buy from people they like AND respect, and they will send everyone they know to someone they respect AND love!

But remember, without your customer, none of this is possible. If you don't lead with your heart, as in, "I'm only going to do this because it benefits me right now and puts money in my pocket today. To hell with the customer," sales is not going to be very easy on you, and any really serious long-term success will continually elude you. Customer service is something that you do for people, and without an intention to service the buyer, there's nothing memorable or valuable about what you're providing him or her. Customers can buy stuff anywhere, but excellent customer service before and after the sale is a truly valuable commodity.

Duane Brain Tip

Reader, when it comes to most people's expectations regarding customer service, there are three things to consider:

1. Time has value, so make good use of your customer's time, keep things moving, and maintain good FLOW;

2. People expect accessibility to you, your management, and to information both during and after the sale;

3. People like to have fun, and, as they say, time flies when you're having fun! When you think about it, you don't work in the sales department. You actually work in the customer service department. The more customer service you can bring to people before, during and after delivery, the more successful you will be.

"Serve them while you sell them, and if you can help enough people get what they want, you'll get everything that you want!"
—*Zig Ziglar*

Of course, in the sales training business, there are many ways to verbalize this approach to customer service. It has been referred to as, "The road to the sale," "Selling steps," and "The path to success."

Some people say to just follow the basics. My thought on these "basics" is that they make less of the sales profession in general. Professional sales is not a "basic" career; it is very involved, involves a lot of skill, and requires a high level of commitment. The fact is, many more salespeople could be much more successful than they currently are.

Selling is not just running down a checklist until the customer buys. If it were that simple, all you would have to do is meet people and tell them, "Listen, Mister. We're going to go through a checklist, and when we get to number eleven, if all goes well, you're going to buy it. Make sense?" What if someone had a question about their trade-in earlier in the process than you normally like to address it? If you are a rigid "road to the sale" salesperson, you would have to say something like, "Mr. or Mrs. Buyer, on my sales checklist, it clearly states that your question is addressed in step nine, but we're actually only on step two right now. We'll get to that in about ninety-five minutes, so please bear with me." Chances are, your customer would walk out way before you got to Step Nine.

The real-world road to a sale is not straight. It's a bumpy, curvy road, full of potholes and detours, with green, yellow, and red lights. A rigid list of sales steps won't work on every customer because each person's buying steps and habits are different—especially A.G.

Duane Brain Tip

Reader, we know that years ago, B.G., our customers had to go from store to store to get even basic information, so they would show up "just looking". "Tire kickers" and "be-backs" dominated our traffic FLOW; closing some-one on the first visit was unusual. As we get further and further into our current era—A.G.—most of our traffic is very closable on the first visit because they come in transaction ready after they have already done their tire kicking online. They can even get frustrated if they are unable to solidify their transaction right then and there.

The fact of the matter is that most of your walk-in traffic has shown up transaction ready, believing they are ready to buy now. Today, the sale goes to the salesperson who makes the fewest mistakes.

If you view the path to success as a stock chart, you will see that it never goes in a straight line for any extended period. There are good months and bad months. The path to success is rough and rocky, but don't despair; if you pull back and take a look at things, you should be able to see a general trend that your numbers are getting better overall, especially if you know you are getting better every day.

One way of looking at the sales process is by comparing it to a jigsaw puzzle. I call it a sales puzzle. Why a puzzle? Well, a puzzle comes in a box that has a picture on the outside showing you how it is supposed to look when the pieces are all put together. When a person comes in to purchase a vehicle, they have a buying puzzle they're trying to put together, which is how they would like things to be by the time they're done. But the buyer's puzzle and the seller's puzzle don't always mix, and they don't always match. The name of the game today is not so much a checklist-style road to a sale, but rather an attempt to put together a puzzle with both yourself and your buyer. I would also suggest that the Internet has simplified things drastically for us. Most consumers today have only a four piece puzzle: the vehicle, their trade, the money, and the person from whom to buy it. So simplify the sale.

Like a real puzzle, a sales puzzle doesn't come with instructions on the puzzle box requiring you to put it together in any specific, step by step manner. Sometimes, you're lucky enough to open the box and find that some of the pieces are already together. This would equate to things your buyer had done to sell and close themselves before they came into your dealership. At the end of the day, you have to put together a puzzle that fits for both you and the buyer.

While most of your buyers do some extensive "tire-clicking" (virtual tire kicking) before they come in, and because they can double-check everything you tell them right in front of you on their mobile computer they also use as a phone (aka smartphone), you have to be spot on throughout. Give yourself the latitude to be able to freestyle a little in the way you handle things as they come up. Just continually assess the situation and ask yourself, "What should be my next step with this particular buyer?"

Top salespeople ask themselves during the sale, "What next sales step will build value for me, my company, or my product?" or, "Will it be an effective use of both my and my customer's time?" or "Would it build trust, credibility, or perceived service?" If they believe the answer is yes, off they go to do it. Another question is, "Would it create a sense of urgency or interest—without lying of course—or might it reduce the buyer's anxiety?" If whatever you're considering does any of these things, it is probably a valuable next step.

I believe some steps are more important than others. Top salespeople engage in the most important steps all the time and fill in gaps with the other things. They may even cover multiple steps at the same time. For example, when I'm selling cars, I usually devalue the trade and assess their buying urgency while I look at the customer's car. I'll also qualify a customer financially using price and payment ranges. I build value in the new car, find out if everyone who needs to be there is there and build rapport with them all while I'm doing the walk around of the new car. I have very simple and concrete word tracks that allow me to do all these things simultaneously to maximize my FLOW.

If you can overlap or do two or more steps at the same time rather than drag them out as individual steps on that road to a sale, you're going to find you'll save some time and help these transaction ready buyers who come in to get things done quickly by use of FLOW and momentum.

In my opinion, the following are the five important, measurable customer service sales steps you can use to actually and quickly qualify a buyer in today's market.

Your Five Most Important Sales Steps:

1. Confirmed Appointments

Solid confirmed appointments are absolutely angelic. That's why my first question is, "Do you or your company use an appointment board?" I'm not referring to just an electronic reminder system but to an actual physical appointment board that you can see and touch and that is prominently located in your office, the showroom, the manager's office, or somewhere else. The idea here is that if it's in front of you, you're more inclined to focus on it. If it's only on your smartphone or computer, when you minimize your screen, you reduce your attention and pressure on it, and that's not what we want. I believe in appointment boards that are there for the entire floor of salespeople to see all day long. Whereas deliveries are like the rear view mirror, appointments are your front window. With that in mind, what's more important: where you've been, or where you're going?

My next question is, "Do you have a personal paper appointment calendar?" Same basic psychology. What's new is not always better. Sure, I use reminders on my smartphone and PC, but I also have a paper appointment calendar. As a matter of fact, my paper appointment calendar is open regardless of where I am doing my work, and right now it is open beside me here in the Rochester, Minnesota airport. That paper calendar is open all the time because filling it up is my most important sales step. Top business and salespeople aren't just focused on appointments—they are obsessed with them.

Let's look at two different quick responses salespeople may have to the question, "How many appointments do you have?"

One salesperson may respond, "I think I had two so far this week, and I might have a couple in the next three or four days."

Salesperson Two says, "I've had three appointments this week; two have shown up, one has not. Of the two who showed up, I've closed one, and delivery is set for Friday. I did not close the other one who came, but he is slated to come back tomorrow. Of the one who did not make it, I've got an appointment already rebooked with him for Saturday. I have four more appointments for the rest of the week, and here are the names, dates, times and situations for each one."

Salesperson One doesn't seem to think that appointments are important. But in the case of the second salesperson, if he/she, or his/her management team, can give you those details regarding appointments quickly and off the cuff, I can tell that it's important for them and that they also focus on it. I can also predict the level of success they will have for the week.

Duane Brain Tip

Reader, a great week is just a bunch of great days stuck together. A great month is caused by a bunch of great weeks. A great year happens after you've had some great months, and a great life is the result of many great years. It all starts with you making a commitment today to have better days—and better sales days are created when you have appointments in your calendar!

Booking Appointments That Show Up

While we're on the subject of appointments, I also want to quickly touch on something else of importance, which is how to effectively book your appointments.

Don't make your appointments by saying, "Come on in at any time," or "I'm available all afternoon," or "I'm here tomorrow from 9-3p.m."

The buyer might say, "Can I come in around 4p.m.?"

Don't respond, saying, "Yes, 4pm should work just fine; I'm here all day," with no attempt to move them to a slightly different specific time or even check on your appointment calendar. That just decreases your value substantially as it indicates to them that you aren't busy.

If you're not busy, the subconscious inference is that you must not be very good. Then thoughts such as, *Your prices must be too high*, *Your trades are too low*, *You provide poor customer service* or *Your product isn't great*, can too easily creep into your customer's mindset.

If you're not busy, fake it until you make it! If you're good, you're going to be busy. So it's very important that you provide the illusion of choice and also the illusion of being busy even if you're not. Play a little hard to get when it comes to booking appointments, and you will book more—and more appointments who show. There's a big difference between booking appointments and booking appointments who show up. Scheduling appointments is easy to do because some customers will readily agree to a loose appointment just to get you off the phone, but getting people to show up is an entirely different technique.

Appointment Lockdown

In the back of this book, you will find the "Appointment Lockdown"—a list of some bullet points and ideas on how you can become an appointment-focused sales professional, how to book odd time appointments (which are sticky and more often kept), how to confirm your appointments, and how to follow up with your no-shows.

The basic difference between a "phone chump" and a "phone champ" is that when taking phone calls, phone chumps give all the exact information and prices on the phone. They're like walking, talking brochures. They may sometimes ask for a name and number, and they may occasionally book an appointment, or at least try to.

A phone champ, on the other hand, will try to avoid giving too much exact product and price information on the phone, will always ask for a name and number(s), and he will always try to book an appointment for a particular time.

By understanding and mastering the above differences in technique, you can shift your personal center of gravity on the phone and become much more successful. Act like a phone champ, and you will get the results that you deserve.

Duane Brain Tip

Reader, phone and Internet traffic is rising and so is their level of seriousness. If you have a so-called fear of the phone, you will also have a fear of paying the rent and retiring when and how you want to! I take and make lots of sales calls when training on-site at my clients' dealerships, for all brands and in all markets. I am fantastic on the phones. Give me a chance to prove it, while training or in a sales challenge, at your dealership.

2. PROPER CHECKING-IN OF THEIR TRADE WHEN YOU ARE SELLING CARS

This is perhaps the most important, misunderstood and poorly utilized piece of your sales puzzle!

The trade-in makes car sales a unique business, and it is also why negotiating will never leave our industry, as the trade value is always a subjective number. When you sell cars, and your buyer has a trade-in vehicle, it is important to check it in properly. There are many people in car sales who just fill out a form or document, enter something into a computer, bring the keys to the appraiser and say, "I need an appraisal."

Duane Brain Tip

Reader, to be clear, the "trade check-in" is a preliminary inspection of the car trade-in done by the salesperson. It is for the salesperson to gather more DNA (Dominant Needs Analysis) as well as to get clarity on their DBM's (Dominant Buying Motives), the person doing the market assessment (for collateral information), and it allows the customer to start emotionally detaching from their vehicle as they begin seeing it from another's eyes.

I would also like to note that you should always inspect and check-in the trade BEFORE the demonstration drive! This will give you even more control and information about your buyer, and make building value in the new car that much easier when comparing the new car to their trade during the demonstration drive. It will also give your management more time to evaluate it and increase your closing ratios substantially as they submit the car to you earlier in the sale!

Sometimes, the sales manager will ask, "Where's the car? What personal effects are in and on the car? How much gas is in it? Has it been cleaned out? What color is the car? What's the exact odometer? What's wrong with the car?" and the sales rep shrugs his shoulders and responds, "I don't know. What does it matter? I just need an appraisal."

If you can't answer those details, then I know you haven't actually seen the vehicle. This means you missed some DNA (Dominant Needs Analysis) that you could have noticed and used had you taken the time to look at their car. You can pick up vital information that will help your sale by briefly inspecting a customer's trade-in before you pass the information on to the person who actually evaluates its market value. Let me elaborate on a few examples I made earlier:

Bumper stickers are great indications of people's personality types. They also clue you in on what you should avoid discussing with them while also working as subject matter to help you build rapport. Items hanging from the rear-view mirror will give you insights as well.

When you open the trunk to check for water leaks or any damage, be alert to any shopping brochures or family, work or hobby items in there. All of this information creates different opportunities to get to know each other even better.

It's OK to be a little nosy when you're inspecting the car as it may give you indications on what you need to do today to gain their business.

Then there are other indications you should be alert to. For example, when their current car is perfectly clean and has almost no gas in it, that's a clear signal that they are planning on getting rid of it and getting into a new car very soon. If you haven't properly checked in their trade-in, you are at a disadvantage in understanding your buyer. What does it mean to properly check-in their trade-in? Let me give you an example:

"Mr. Buyer, let's do a quick inspection of your vehicle together. I don't do the actual market assessment, but I do collect information about your car so I can pass it over to management. Help me sell your car to management so she can do an accurate equity review. Let's go look at it!"

Then you and your buyer go to the car, and you casually do a silent walk-around. Make sure you don't frown at problems too much or smile at things that look great; it's a brief, poker-faced walk around the car. If you see a lot of damages, don't touch them; that's the manager's job. Just pause, look at them, and then move on. They will notice that you saw and usually have a comment about how the damage occurred. If you want to bring your smartphone into the equation to take pictures of the trim, emblems, tires and rims, the body from two opposite corners, the engine, the VIN numbers on the door and the front window, the odometer and engine, it's going to bring a lot more credibility to your assessment. And their reactions to all this will help you assess their level of urgency. You can do the same with any product trade-in.

Once you've finished that, get all the documentation—the title/ownership, the insurance, their driver's license and the keys. Don't forget to ask them if they brought both sets of keys or key fobs with them: if they did, they are probably ready to buy right now.

Duane Brain Tip

Reader, when I'm selling cars and booking appointments, I always ask if this newer car is an addition or replacement for their current car (but not if they will be trading something in). Then, when reconfirming the appointment, I mention, "Please have your car cleaned out, bring both key fobs, and park it in front of the building on the far left side so we can spend some time assessing it. When you come in, please hand me your keys, registration, insurance, and driver's license so we can really move things along for you." Try this yourself, and you will be shocked how many people will happily comply. When they do, you are looking at a transaction ready buyer whom you have converted into a willing participant of your full sales process.

If they give you all the keys—with their house keys and such on the ring—tell them, "For my peace of mind and yours, I don't need all your keys; I only need the keys to your car." Then you physically remove the car key from the ring. That might be a bit of an emotional moment for the buyer, as it may be the first time in a long while that the car key has been separate from the rest. Also, by not having their house keys, you are making sure you're not liable for anything that could go wrong at their home for the next few days.

While looking at the vehicle, ask questions like:

"Have you recently had it professionally appraised?"

"What are your current payments on the vehicle, and how many do you have left?"

"How did you get those payments so low?"

"Did you buy it new or used?"

"What did you like about the car?"

"What didn't you like about the car?"

"Does anyone else drive it or sit in it often?"

"What do you or anyone else usually keep in the trunk?"

"Will our police report, accident or insurance searches pull any incidents?"

There are a lot of wants, needs and financial information you can gather, but the two most powerful questions I'd like you to remember to ask when you properly check that car in are:

"Just to be clear, you are looking to replace this with something like the X model, is that correct?" and, "How soon could we have your car if the numbers worked out?"

The answers to those questions, when asked at their vehicle, will tell you about their transaction readiness. That is what I mean by properly checking in and checking out the trade-in.

You can also increase connection and credibility when you inspect the car. By showing interest in the vehicle, you show your buyer that you are not only interested in the car but also in them. If you have a couple of appointments in a day and check in a couple of trade-ins with a proper inspection process, you're probably going to sell at least one vehicle.

Duane Brain Tip

Reader, I strongly suggest you give your buyer a finishing statement when walking away from their trade, such as this: "Well, logically, your car will never have less miles on it, be newer or be in better shape than today, and we know market values fluctuate all the time. Isn't it crazy to see what some people are ASKING online? Maybe one day, someone will invent a used car website that prints checks. Hahaha. Let's see if we can make things happen for you in the real world today!"

3. A Great Demonstration

Another excellent sales step is to do a dynamic presentation and demonstration. Have them try the product out. In the case of selling a car, don't just flip them a key and tell them to take a peak themselves or go for a test drive. If you do, you miss out on some of your best opportunities for getting a sale, and you also waste a lot of time because you could have accomplished multiple goals while in the car with them. You have to be with your clients when they test the product.

If you are selling a car, good customer service means you should be in the car with them to build extra value in the product. In the case of selling a house, you wander around the house with them. You're there to answer any questions, to go through features and benefits, and build rapport. No matter what it is that you are selling, if it can be demonstrated, you should be there, moving things along properly. You stay with the customer and have him or her try it out, whether it be a car or a vacuum cleaner.

The idea is to talk a bit more at the beginning of the demonstration and a little bit less later on, giving the customer a chance to really understand, appreciate and feel the item. Demonstration is fundamental.

If you just throw someone a key to a car or walk off while someone tries out a product, you're being incompetent and uncaring as a salesperson. That is just awful customer service. In my opinion, you should be terminated for not being there for the demonstration. There may be occasions when the client might want to be left alone with their spouse or family to review things, but this would only be permitted after you have done an initial outstanding orientation presentation to the primary buyers, and with management's permission. Just remember, your product knowledge and presentation should focus on the features and equipment a customer can see, feel and use. For many reasons, the "unseen" specifications are best addressed using literature and online information as provided by your manufacturer.

As said earlier, "Ms. Buyer, anything I can't read off our product will be verified at my workstation."

If you just throw someone a key to a car or walk off while someone tries out a product, you're being incompetent and uncaring as a salesperson.

Lazy or unthinking salespeople who don't give their customers a fantastic product demonstration are a liability to themselves and to the company they work for. We know their closing ratio and gross profits will be lower than they could be because an interactive and enthusiastic product presentation is what sells the product and also sells the customer on you. If you're not there to answer the little questions that always come up, appropriate sales closes will be few and far between. It costs your company real money to get customers to walk through the front door.

Negligent or ignorant salespeople who don't, won't or can't show their products to their customers in a professional manner should be restricted from getting any traffic until they are trained correctly. If they still refuse to do their job, they should be written up, and if necessary, terminated or have their sales license revoked. Why wait for them to fail on their own?

Speaking of sales licenses, here is something funny about needing a sales license if your region requires one:

As salespeople, we're under a lot of pressure to be professional and ethical due to legal requirements, government regulations, competition, and the need for good customer service by our companies and manufacturers. No matter what is being sold, the salesperson can sometimes get a bad rap. The odd horror story makes the newspaper, and, just like lawyers, if there's one bad salesman, everyone else is painted with the same brush. However, nowadays, I would suggest that if there is going to be some ethical difficulty in the sale, it is more often on the part of the buyer.

If I had a dime for every time a buyer told me something that wasn't true, or outright malicious or vindictive, I would be doing okay financially just on the profits of that alone. I know we're in a market where salespeople have to be monitored and/or licensed, and that's a good thing, but I honestly do believe that customers should have to acquire a buyer's license to purchase anything. After all, a sale is a two-way street.

To get a buyer's license to buy a car, a prospective buyer should have to study some material and then go down to one's local government office and take a test on the realities of the car business today. It's important for consumers to understand what it takes to run a business and to stay in business. What the overhead is, the risk and capital required, what an invoice actually represents, what the real costs are to actually do business, what the profit margins are actually like, what pressures exist from competition around us, what the Internet has done to the car sales industry, what it is like to deliver the products, and the technical complexities involved in servicing them—these should all be part of the buyer's initiation. But the buyer doesn't have to do or know anything about the real buying/sales process. They can be as educated, uneducated, misinformed and confused about the product and process as they want to be.

Let's imagine for a moment that they did have to take a buyer's test. Once they had passed their test and paid the fee for a buyer's license, they'd be permitted to come into a store or dealership and talk to a salesperson. And when they do, you could say, "Great, I just need your buyer's license and then we can move forward." If they don't have it, they could complete it on-site, or you could just send them on their way to go study for it and take that written test—perhaps acting as their sponsor to ensure they come back.

I am dead serious when I say this should happen. Just like a fishing or hunting license, a lot of these licensing offices and committees are supposed to be non-profit, but they require personnel, offices, have overhead costs and so on. Imagine what kinds of facilities they could build, and just think what it would do for their revenue streams if there were a real requirement for consumers to get a buyer's license? I think that this is as valid as today's requirement for sales licenses. It may sound like wishful thinking, but I think it's a great idea.

From a sales perspective, how great would it be to have a customer walk in with a buyer's license that they had to work and pay for? That would be a fairly strong indication of a buyer, no? Take that idea to your next council meeting!

4. Round Number Ranges

Duane Brain Tip

Reader, this is a crucial step and will be a game changer for many of you if you do it before the demonstration drive. If you skip this crucial step, staying off price or getting lazy and asking dumb things like, "How much do you want to pay, and what's your budget?" you will be punished with lost sales, reduced profit and wasted time for both you and your customer.

All prospective buyers get verbal *round prices* or *payment ranges* before the driving demonstration. What this means is the salesperson gives a rounded figure or payment range instead of an exact price. Round number ranges are a way of qualifying people on whether they can afford the product (or an alternative) without getting into exact figures. So, as mentioned in an earlier chapter, you don't want to stay off price, but you should stay off exact price.

When you get a green light from your customer on the equipment, price and payment ranges before the demonstration drive, your FLOW will increase dramatically, as will your profit and closing ratios!

Giving a number range sounds something like this:

"Mr. or Mrs. Buyer, the car that you're looking at has been built to sell for X dollars, as equipped. We'll double check the exact pricing and programs back at my workstation. Just so you know, a nicely equipped model in this line-up starts off at this amount (lowest priced model with the fewest features), and a fully equipped model goes all the way up to this amount (highest priced model with the most features)." Pause. "Do you have any questions on either the features or the price?" (Use the words "features and equipment" because that is what the buyer will use, so those words build value. The word "options" costs money, and, like an add-on, it will reduce value).

By calmly disclosing that price review as a round number range, people will do one of three things:

I. They will say something like, "I think we're good. We'll just double-check the final numbers when we get inside." This means you're on the right product, amounts and features.

II. Others will ask something like, "What would it be without the XYZ feature?" or, "What's in the lower priced car?" This tells you they want to spend less money and/or they may not need that much equipment.

III. Some people will ask about the higher priced item, which means they might have more money and may want to get more bells and whistles.

Just by disclosing a price range and deflecting the specifics to my workstation, I get the elephant out of the room and can start building value as well as begin to qualify the buyer for the right product. Because so many consumers today don't actually pay cash for their more expensive goods, and they will most likely be making monthly payments, it's important you have a rule of thumb that allows you to convert price to payment and payment to price.

For car loans, a good rule of thumb is that monthly payments are typically about $200/month for every $10,000 in total borrowed on a short-term five-year loan. This is easy to remember and calculate up or down while you're on your feet.

Duane Brain Tip

Reader, by using a short term as a starting point for your round numbers, it gives you lots of room for front or back-end profit and the flexibility to reduce payments by extending the term, asking for more money down, or switching to a different product.

So, for car sales, rounded-off rubber payments would go something like this: "Mr. Buyer, the vehicle you're looking at is about $40,000. On a short-term, five-year loan, $40,000 would be about $800ish a month, or a little less than half that every two weeks on a bi-weekly loan, but that's over just five years and not an exact quote. So if we extended the term, the payment would decrease. Do you have any questions on those payment ranges or the vehicle itself? Are we in the right ballpark?"

And they again may either ask about the lower payment or the higher payment. If they are quite out of alignment with what a realistic payment range is, based on the terms you know you can go down to, you may have to discuss other terms such as leasing, more money down, or even a different kind of product. You might have to suggest a different model year, a company demonstration model, something with different equipment, perhaps an entirely different model, a used car, or something with totally different incentives.

Once you get comfortable with these averages and your products, inventory and programs, your ability to discuss round number ranges on your feet will help you build value with your transaction ready buyers quickly and effectively and will set you apart from the price avoiders.

Sales people today face the additional challenges of dealing with shrinking attention spans, decreasing basic functional math abilities, and the misinformation and disinformation on the Internet. So being able to reset and refocus someone on a product in the right price and payment range early in the sale is now a non-negotiable skill set that sales people must have. As another option, the simple calculator on your smartphone can save a sale. Just take the price of the product (including approximate taxes, fees and maybe interest), and divide it by the customers requested payment, and you will have the term of the loan required.

Again, practice common sense here. But this Rubber Payment and Term, when shown on your calculator screen, can bring a whole new level of reality to your situation. "So, Mr. Buyer, you want a payment of $300 a month on this $50,000 truck. No problem. Let's just add a bit for taxes and fees, and then divide that number by $300 … and … um … we don't offer 200 month financing, which, if I divide by 12, is almost 17 years! So perhaps we need to discuss a realistic term length and how we can lower the balance financed with cash, trade or a different car."

Duane Marino
NAASSA, MarinoTV & TNT
New Paths to Outstanding Success
1-888-735-6275
www.DuaneMarino.com

NAASSA - North American Automotive Sales Success Academy.
MarinoTV - Industry's best on-line sales training resource.
TNT - Traffic Events, Event Sales & BDC for Hire.

You can also be prepared for some customers to ask this question: "Is that your best price?" On MarinoTV, which is my online training portal (www.DuaneMarino.com), I've got lots of great techniques to handle that.

I either deflect this question or turn it into a bit of a joke, or perhaps I'll try to switch or trap them. You have to prepare yourself with an arsenal of answers to questions such as, "Is that your best price?"

One last thought about pricing that can make the difference between closing and losing the sale: closers always determine a customer's buying and urgency intentions before the quote. Losers learn a customer's intentions after the quote.

Set yourself up properly, as your first price quote is your most important price quote. And please, don't stay off price. Just learn to stay off *exact price*.

Duane Brain Tip

Reader, the last thing you want is a surprise credit concern towards the end of your sale, and many people don't really know how or when to bring it up themselves. Here is a great, non-confrontational way to start that conversation early in the sale. Ask your prospect, "Have you already taken the time to arrange your own financing, or would you be curious to see what our lenders could offer you?" The answers they give you to that question will tell you a lot about them and where they are in their buying and credit process.

I offer all my customers a free credit approval as early in the sale as possible. "To save hassle, many people get a pre-approved mortgage before they buy a house; and since a car is your second biggest purchase, I offer the same customer service for free should you be interested. It only takes a few minutes. Do you want to do that or just continue on with the car?" Transaction ready buyers love this, and whoever completes the credit application is buying today from you! So let your customers put this minor decision before their major one, and use credit as a FLOW and closing tool.

5. Follow-up

It is important to follow up with your owners and buyers, but there is a right way and a wrong way to go about this.

You don't want to just call them every few weeks or months with a rote script that you read from, asking for referrals or telling them about some sale. If you do it that way, you don't become valuable or memorable because your calls sound canned and are not enjoyable for your customer. You want to call them and follow up in a way that maintains a REALationship with them. Faking it by using word tracks from your CRM or some training manual is counter-productive to building or maintaining a real rapport. Bear in mind that following up with your owners and following up with your potential, but, yet unclosed, customers who will "be back", are two entirely different situations that we will discuss later.

For the time being, here is a question for you regarding the five most important sales steps of Confirmed Appointments, Proper Check-in of the Trade, Presentations and Demonstrations, Round Number Ranges, and Follow-up: ask yourself, "If this is really the customer service business, how are these all done with Vitamin L *for* your customer and not *to* them?"

Let me share these examples with you of how you can manage common customer questions and justify what you are doing:

Setting an Appointment

The customer asks me: "Duane, why 2:20pm? Why can't I just pop in at any time?"

My response: "Mr./Mrs. Buyer, of course you can just pop in, and I'll do my best to be available, but I might not be. If we book an exact time, I'll be free for you. And since I know that your time is valuable, this way I can serve you better. I'd like to set an exact appointment time to help serve you better and to make sure I'm free for you."

Trade-in

Customer asks: "Why are you taking a few minutes to look at my trade-in? The other dealership just gave us a number—they didn't do all this."

My response: "Mr. Buyer, you obviously didn't do business there, with that person, for a reason. For us to get an accurate market value and give you as much as possible, we need to put some effort into it. That way, we can try to sell my management team on buying your car. More detail equals confidence, and confidence means a better and more accurate number."

Accompanied Test Drive

Customer asks: "Why are you coming for a drive with us?"

My response: "Well, we come for a drive with you to make sure we can answer all of your questions while you are actually driving the vehicle. I'm in the customer service industry, and I wouldn't feel right just throwing you the keys. That would be like a real estate agent pulling up to a house, giving you the keys and saying, 'Just go through the house and tell me what you think.' In my opinion, that's just not good customer service. And it could open us up to liability issues with our insurance company."

Customer says: "We don't want to drive the car."

My response (given with a smile): "To be honest with you, I don't really want to drive it either. I've driven this car many times myself. But I do remember once that I bought a pair of shoes without trying them on. They weren't the right shoes for me, and I couldn't take them back after I wore them. That was only fifty dollars. As a company, we know what kind of decision it is for people to select a car, and we feel better if our customers drive the vehicle the same day they get quotes or make decisions. It's company policy; we want to make sure no one makes any mistakes."

Customer says: "Well I still don't want to drive it." or "We drove it at the other dealership."

My response: "I can't rely on the other dealership to do my job", or "Mr. or Mrs. Buyer, did you drive your last car just *before* you bought it?" This question will give you great information either way and solve your problem.

If they answer, "Yes, we did," you can say, "Exactly. Let's just go for a spin."

If they say, "No, we didn't," you can say, "Great, I know there are a few people out there like that. Let's go work out the numbers and finish this off."

When you recognize that the entire sales process is a sales puzzle and you're not doing everything the same way each time, you will also learn that these five sales steps are the fundamental drivers for your business. Generally, you don't want to skip demonstrations, but there is always the odd person out there who will buy something without testing it out first, just like I often do.

If they entirely bypass the drive somehow and go straight to your office for pricing, excuse yourself to check with management on pricing and availability. Then return to your customer with the key in hand to the truck you are selling. "Ms. Buyer, management will be working on your quote for the next few minutes. Instead of sitting here, let's go sit in the truck to make sure it has everything you expect. Please follow me."

The probability of selling and making some money increases if you can get your customer into the car before you quote exact numbers by bringing their emotions and excitement to a peak.

Talking Price Ranges Early in the Process

Customer asks: "Why the round number range? Can't you give us an exact price?"

My response: "Well, of course I can. I know my numbers have to be competitive. There are a lot of variables involved in that pricing that I'd rather address when we're sitting down face-to-face at my workstation than out here. I just don't want to make any mistakes for you or me, but the range I gave you is reasonably accurate, and this saves time. Are we moving in the right direction? Are we in the right ballpark?"

Customer asks again: "But what can I buy it for?" I would test their commitment to the vehicle and ask them, "Are you looking for the best price, or the best value? Some of our customers start off with this van, but then they buy this other one as they feel it's a better value and has everything they want or need at a similar price. And this other one is our most popular model right now. Can I show it to you?"

If the customer persists aggressively with a comment such as "Value, shmalue … just give me your best price!" I might go into an assertive trap. It wouldn't be out of line at this point to say something like, "We'll always be flexible if you can be reasonable. Are we negotiating right now, yes or no?"

Immediate "Be Back" Follow-Up

Customer asks: "Why are you calling already? We were just in there and haven't made a decision yet."

My response: "I'm just thanking you for taking the time to come into our dealership. I was just wondering if you had any questions for me while things are still fresh in your mind. I want you to know you're valuable to me either way, and Mr. or Mrs. Buyer, we will also service whatever you end up purchasing if we can." And then you go back to the conversation of whatever item you're trying to sell them.

The bottom line here is that you have to learn how to serve people while selling them, and be able to justify it! Without question, this requires you to be able to bring in a little bit of Vitamin L (Love) into it.

You can do an excellent job with those five sales steps and by being flexible enough to be able to modify your process a little on a customer-by-customer basis. Customer service—everything we do begins and ends with it.

And remember, as I've said, thanks to the Internet, your customer's buying puzzle only has 4 pieces by the time they show up at your store: the car, their trade, the salesperson, and the money. Make sure you isolate which ones are the most important to address, and spend the most time and energy on those!

CHAPTER 9

Power #2: Your Power of Communication

Your next sales power is the Power of Communication to Build Relationships. An odd little sentence to remember is, "We cannot NOT communicate." Your body language, mannerisms, the way you talk, your posture and facial expressions are always communicating something to the people around you. If you're a people watcher, then you will enjoy observing these social cues in others in your daily life

Additionally, it is impossible to not communicate with yourself. There is always some thought process, some feeling or reaction going on in your mind or body. Understanding and improving one's ability to control the power of communication is essential to improving oneself and one's relationships with others.

When you communicate, it isn't usually the exact words you say that people will remember. Rather, people will remember how you made them feel by how you said it. The emotional message *is* the message. Communication is often controlled through the use of questions and the type of questions one asks. Listening is also a powerful ingredient to communication and should not be neglected in any study of the subject.

Listening is also a powerful ingredient to communication and should not be neglected in any study of the subject.

The physical manner in which you communicate—your center of gravity (whether you lean forward or back, off to one side or the other), your face, your eyes, your proximity to the other person, which way your feet, shoulders and chin point, hand gestures, tone, inflection, facial expressions, and so on—can enhance or detract from the quality of your message. A great communicator will also pay attention to those same signals in the person they are communicating with.

If you become aware of these elements, you will have total control over yourself and excellent control of your communications with your prospective buyers. Remember, everything in life can be ingrained by habit, including your communication skills. If you haven't really given a lot of thought to these skills previously, write them down on paper and place them on your desk so you can become actively aware of them. In doing so, you may find out, as I did years ago, that you have some communication habits that are not appropriate or beneficial to the selling process.

To help you better relate to your customer, you should pay attention to four things. I call this getting a buyer's FORM. F.O.R.M. stands for Family, Occupation, Recreation and Money.

Let's take up "F" first.

"F" is for Family

You want to know these things about your prospect:

- Do they have children?
- Are they married?
- Are they divorced?
- What's their family situation? (Who's really in charge and has the final say?)
- How do they seem to act and react with their family?
- Do they enjoy having a family, or do they act like they don't?

One thing to understand about people and their personality traits, including what their wants, needs and interests are, is that it's not always necessarily about making a connection. Being able to make a strong connection is very valuable, but it is also important to avoid accidentally *disconnecting* from people by offending them. The way to avoid this is to pick up on their values and interests to ensure you don't inadvertently upset them.

When you talk favorably about things they don't like, you can actually cause a breakdown in rapport. People tend to buy from others who are similar to themselves in terms of their likes, values, etc. When you come across as liking things that they might take offense to, it can create an immediate and sometimes insurmountable difference between the two of you. Understanding their FORM isn't just about connecting; it's also about carefully making sure you don't disconnect from or offend others.

People seldom have the exact same opinions and have very different values about politics, sex and religion, so those topics should be avoided.

When you talk favorably about things they don't like, you can actually cause a breakdown in rapport.

"O" is for Occupation

- What do they do for a living?
- How long have they been doing that?
- Do they like what they do?

"R" is for Recreation

By recreation, we essentially mean hobbies. What do they enjoy doing?

Sports? Fishing? Taking photos? Dancing?

You should try to tie your product presentation into those interests. Hobbies could also overlap into work and family.

"M" is for Money

With most of your clients, you will never actually know just how much money they have. This is not a topic people have been educated in to share willingly, and, for the most part, it's none of your business. Just make sure you don't judge a book by its cover. It's not uncommon for people with money to act, dress, and walk in different ways than their financial situation would seem to dictate. Sometimes, this is done intentionally to throw you off their scent or just to see if you'll prequalify them.

Most self-made millionaires didn't have money at one time. And many are like me in that I often want to see if the salesperson is going to prequalify me or treat me poorly because they think I don't have the means to move forward. So, few financial signals are sent out to the salesperson. We're sensing your character and motivation. Are you just after the money, or do you seem to genuinely want to help people find what they're looking for?

On the other hand, many people who don't have much money will go out of their way to dress and act as if they are wealthy. They'll say and do things to try to make you think they have more money than they actually do. The surface appearance of wealth is never a good idea and can lead to many mistakes in prequalifying people.

Duane Brain Tip

Reader, people are tribal with regard to many things, including how they relate to money. Having worked in sales in many diverse markets, I have met many farmers who are multi-millionaires, yet who prefer to dress and drive cars that would make one think they are broke. Conversely, many high-density urban dwellers are broke, and yet they like to dress and drive cars to make one believe they are multi-millionaires. With that in mind, never make the mistake of prequalifying people financially only on superficial clues. Instead, try to figure out what feelings and associations they have connected to their money, and how much money they feel is appropriate to spend on your product or one like it. Your verbal review of round price ranges, rubber payments and offers to use your lenders will give you valuable feedback regarding the financial aspects of your buyer and the transaction.

Some people with a lot of money may not feel it's appropriate to spend money on the type of product you are selling. On the other hand, people who don't have a lot of money may love the product you sell for many emotional or social reasons and are willing to put a substantial amount towards them.

Understanding their motivations can give you an advantage over your competition and can ensure that you don't make critical mistakes with your prospects.

Also, if your product involves financing of any type, please refer to my statements earlier about how to gently and in a non-confrontational way bring up that topic sooner, rather than later. I have, on occasion, used tools like Google Earth to get an idea of where and how my customers live, and even what their workplace looks like. There are so many tools available to us now through the Internet that can help us connect with and understand our buyers. Use whatever ones you can, as long as you stay within ethical and legal boundaries.

Mirroring People

If you were to Google or YouTube the topic "Mirroring People," you would find information about a number of different psychological disciplines on the subject. "Mirroring" refers to deliberately following along with what the other person is doing, and mimicking them in a subtle manner. They laugh, so you chuckle. They frown, and you turn a lip down. It's something you're probably doing naturally to some extent already, but there's a real art to mastering it. If you pay attention to such interactions, you may start to notice that when someone really likes somebody and is comfortable with them, their mannerisms will be very similar to the other person's.

The word for this is "entrainment". Entrainment means to follow along with similar characteristics and match the other person. If one person leans back, then the other will do so as well. If one person giggles, the other person smiles.

Conversely, if someone doesn't like the other person or is having a bad day, they may do the opposite of what the other person does. For example, one laughs while the other person keeps a straight face. This sends out a signal: "I'm not enjoying my time with you right now, and I want it to be over as soon as possible. I'm breaking the dance."

The art of mirroring people is important, especially if you want them to connect with you rapidly on a subconscious level.

Five Personality Types

Another thing that can help you effectively connect with someone is being alert to the type of personality the person has and how it influences the way they behave and make decisions. There are five primary personality types that I will briefly address, and although they go by many different titles, I will go with the ones I use. These personality profiles are as follows: Amiable, Expressive, Analytical, Drivers, and the Chameleon. The manner in which you effectively communicate with each one of these personalities is different and can become a deciding factor in whether you will successfully move towards a sale or not. Self-awareness is also vital, so it's important that you also try to identify your own dominant personality profile as you will find that you have a bit of all of them in you. Do you relate primarily to other people as more of an Amiable or an Expressive, and do you make decisions as more of an Analytical or a Driver?

You can't mirror people well until you realize what you project.

Amiable Communicators

Amiable people are generally low key. If they're truly amiable, they will have an almost suspiciously-pleasing personality and will often dress in loose fitting, muted and plain clothes. They like to fit in and mix with the masses. They'll sound very polite and interested in what you have to say even when they are not actually interested at all.

Amiable people don't like getting attention because attention can lead to a potential conflict. They'll go out of their way to avoid conflict. They'll agree with you even when they don't really. They'll say they'll be back when they have no intention of returning. They just want to get out of there without a hassle.

Amiable people don't complain; they just don't come back. They are so low key that you always have to ask kind and specific questions when selling to them, and you must also mirror that relaxed, polite personality type. Of course we will all assume a more amiable position when we are trying to avoid a confrontation, but when this is the trait that dominates someone's behavior and dress patterns, know that you are dealing with an amiable personality type, so act accordingly.

Amiable salespeople get along well with most customers but usually find it challenging to close the sale.

Expressive Communicators

On the other hand, the expressive personality will be a more aggressive communicator. Expressive people are usually flashier than those who aren't, can be a bit flirty, like to joke, and don't mind getting all the attention. Because they like to attract attention, they will sometimes do things that generate negative attention. But for them, even negative attention is better than no attention. With that in mind, you're going to have to pick up your energy level quite a bit when you sell to an expressive personality.

Again, you will see patterns of this in your friends, family, customers and yourself. A good exercise would be to discover which type you gravitate towards more naturally. Expressive salespeople have a high level of enthusiasm but can put their foot in their mouths.

Duane Brain Tip

Reader, it's also important to know that people can display very different communication styles depending on their environment and how comfortable they are. So be prepared to shift your mirroring style to whatever communication style your "target" is using at that time!

The Buyer's Decision-Making Process

There are two types of decision-making processes that we all have. However, we will lean more towards either being analytical or a driver.

Analytical Decision Makers

The analytical personality is all about facts and figures, numbers and details. They make their decisions based strictly on logic. They're unemotional decision-makers who thrive on giving and getting information.

In selling to this type of personality, you don't want to say things that you can't prove because providing verifiable information is one of the key ways to connect and gain credibility with analytical-type people. They can take a longer time to sell, and you may have to be very patient and thorough when bringing them through the process. You should be prepared to back up and prove everything you say in writing or with visuals, as this makes your data verifiable. Round numbers, rubber payments, price ranges, ballpark figures, "-ishs", approximate specifications and uncertain availability times are not acceptable for long with true "analyticals". They have little tolerance for gray areas—it's either black or white. They want exact details.

Analytical salespeople are great with details and product knowledge but can be guilty of giving too much information.

Drivers

Another personality type is the driver. Drivers are a bit more assertive, and they can be somewhat louder. They'll often park their cars more aggressively than an analytical personality type. They may wear power suits, and they love getting attention, because to them, it is about the perception of dominance.

In selling to this type, you have to be careful: if you're too assertive with a driver, they will raise their assertion level until you're in an argument. They can be competitive to the point of becoming combative.

However, if you're too submissive with the driver type, they will actually want to bypass you and go straight to a manager because they don't like dealing with meek or weak people. With this type, you'll always have to adjust your energy level to make sure you don't offend, or alternatively, lose credibility with them.

In comparison, an analytical type is a slow and unemotional decision maker, whereas a driver is a fast, emotional decision maker. Which one describes you best in most situations? Does the type or price of the product you are buying change your decision-making style?

Driver salespeople love to take charge and move through the sale but may be accused of being too aggressive.

Chameleon

There is a fifth personality type: the chameleon. Chameleons change their personality according to who they are around. If you're an amiable person, they will act amiably. If you're an energetic and expressive person, chameleons will pick up on your expressiveness and energy and play off of it. Basically, chameleons quickly and comfortably become like the person they're with.

Over time, your goal as an effective salesperson should be to become more and more like a chameleon. Ideally, you should be able to get to a point where you can easily be any and all of the previously listed personality types. You will be most successful in sales if your own personality type can align to the situation you find yourself in.

I can instantly adapt to the personalities I am around, and the only two factors that will impede this for me are if I am very tired or if I genuinely don't respect the person I am with.

Chameleon salespeople have also learned how to adapt and moderate their own strengths and weaknesses during the sale.

Two Additional Conditions of Personality

There are two other conditions of personality that should be mentioned here because there are a lot of misunderstandings surrounding them. These are the more common distinctions of the introvert versus the extrovert.

Introverts & Extroverts

In a nutshell, introverts are people who recharge their batteries by themselves. Extroverts are people who recharge their batteries around other people.

An introvert in a people business such as sales can still have great social skills at work and be very effective at selling.

But, at the end of the day, he or she chooses to relax by him or herself. The introvert prefers smaller groups or solitude over larger gatherings.

An extrovert, on the other hand, can have the same social and communication skills, but when she's done with work and ready to unwind, she prefers to do so in the company of more people.

Sometimes, introverts and extroverts don't really understand each other.

The two most successful salespeople I've ever met fall within both extremes of this spectrum. Ironically, they didn't live very far from each other.

How do you recharge your own batteries? Do you prefer to be alone, or would you rather participate in big groups and surround yourself with people? By this observation, you now know whether you're introverted or extroverted. Neither is better than the other; it's simply good to know yourself and be more self-aware of your personality. This way, you can better understand what comes naturally and comfortably to you and what may need to be worked on and smoothed out.

I am definitely an introvert, or, as some would call it, a "situational extrovert." I love being around people at work and when I feel great, but when I'm not at work, or if I'm tired or don't feel well, I prefer to spend time alone with my family or in very small groups.

Tribal Laws

When you communicate with people, you need to be aware of certain unstated social expectations. "Tribal Laws" are what I call those unspoken agreements between people that govern how they should behave and communicate, and how they are expected to get along with others within their group or cultural area. Such laws are usually pretty straightforward:

- People tend to buy from people they like or respect.
- People tend to like or respect people who are similar to them.
- People tend to like or respect people who seem to like and respect them.
- People tend to like people whom they want to be like.

You can immediately see from the above why the simple act of smiling can be very important. A smile indicates that you like or respect the person you're with, and people tend to act very differently towards you when they feel that you like and respect them.

Duane Brain Tip

Reader, I believe it's a lie that people buy from people whom they like. When selling to someone, it is far more important that your customer respects you than likes you, although both would be ideal. As far as leadership goes, when people like and respect you, they will want to be similar to you and will be more willing to follow you in what you do. And this all begins with you liking and respecting them as well. This is an excellent way to have some influence and leadership at home and work, and to have people look up to you.

Using Colorful Language

Sometimes people are taken aback that I use silly or slightly colorful language in my live seminars. I explain that I deliberately choose to do so for a couple of reasons.

First of all, and bearing in mind that my audience is composed of salespeople, I want to make sure that my audience is thick-skinned and not overly sensitive. If a salesperson is hyper- sensitive, then it's going to be difficult for them to be very successful in this business, or for that matter, to be my customer in a coaching situation.

The second reason I opt for a little colorful language is to loosen everyone up and let them know they can be themselves around me.

However, in a one-on-one conversation, I do not use colorful language. This is because with one-on-ones, you could be dealing with an individual who doesn't like it and rejects you on the spot for that reason alone, ending the sale then and there.

On the other hand, it is interesting to note that some customers will use a lot of profanity once they get comfortable with you. People come in all types and character, and you can easily assume something about your customer that ends up being completely off the mark. You may be dealing with an 80-year-old woman who is still a brash 28-year-old on the inside. Know that it is the latter whom you're actually talking to. For certain, looks can be deceiving.

It is imperative, then, to learn how to effectively mirror all communication and decision-making styles. If you have someone who uses a lot of profanity, and you don't use some colorful language at least once, that person may grow uncomfortable with you and may not buy the product from you. Language is one of the most important ways that we bond.

Be a chameleon, or you will find you are very limited with your audience of potential prospects. Even if it makes you uncomfortable, find a way to slip in at least one marginally colorful word when a customer is using them a lot with you. If you do it appropriately, it will give you a higher level of rapport with them. It's all about mirroring the person in front of you. Their "tribe"—their family and friends—all probably use the same colorful language once in a while, so they're going to be expecting you to do the same in order for them to feel comfortable with you.

Bonding With Sales Glue

With each thing you do, you either increase the attraction or repulsion factor between yourself and the prospective buyer. There are a couple of aspects that can significantly boost the solidarity of the sales relationships you create. They're like glue because they increase the bond between you and your prospective buyers.

Humor

Do not underestimate the bonding properties of humor. A lot of great chemistry is required for people to genuinely laugh with, and not at, each other. Getting someone to laugh along with you only happens if you have established a real connection or are moving in the direction of one. Anyone who has sold anything can tell you from experience that your profit and closing ratios on customers who are really laughing with you are in a completely different range than the sales you make with people who are not sharing humor with you. The rule of thumb here is to find out as early in the sale as possible where their sense of humor is, and then build upon it. The safest way to do this is to make jokes about yourself first.

For example, if I'm on my game and "feeling it" I use humor in these various ways:

If it's windy, I might take hold of my eyebrows (don't forget, I have a shaved head), and say with a chuckle, "My goodness, is my hair messed up? Do I look okay?"

The rule of thumb here is to find out as early in the sale as possible where their sense of humor is, and then build upon it. The safest way to do this is to make jokes about yourself first.

If it's really sunny, I'll cover my head and go, "Jeez, I'm burning. You look like you'll be all right with your wonderful head of hair, but I think I'll be burning here pretty soon."

Or if it's raining, I'll just wipe the top of my head a little bit and say, with a smirk, "Well I can always squeegee the water off my head, but would you like me to grab you an umbrella?"

By using some simple introductory humor and making fun of myself, there is no way I can ever offend the other person right from the start. If they laugh, (as most people do), I know they have a sense of humor that I can build on, and there is some bonding going on. The sale usually just gets easier from there.

If they don't laugh, I make a mental note and become very careful at any humor I try from that point forward. Some people are very dry, and by being the same, you can create a connection with them. But at least making the effort to find a laugh or a smile with your prospective buyer, and identifying what type of humor they have, is well worth it. A real smile will move you a mile in the progress of your sale.

What evident and likable things about yourself could you joke of?

Duane Brain Tip

Reader, in my personal life, I use outlandish and ridiculous humor to see if I want to spend time with someone. I can find humor in everything, and anyone who is too uptight or intolerant is not a good match for me. I consider both my time and the time of anyone I meet to be very valuable, and bizarre humor is a way for me to quickly filter out people whom I probably wouldn't get along with anyway.

Other Types of Sales Glue

Finding common interests is a great way to create a feeling of familiarity with your buyer, and as I mentioned earlier, being a chameleon will always bring you and your customer closer together.

Duane Brain Tip

Reader, it should go without saying that you should never lie. Communities are small, repeats and referrals are your future, the Internet is pervasive, and death to your sales career through negative posts on Google, Facebook and other social media is not fun.

Also, be competent in your career. If you are new, say so. If you don't know something, compliment the customer with, "That's a great question. Let's find out when we get into the showroom where I can check all my resources."

Covert Rapport and Language Patterns

Another thing you want to develop with your customer is rapport, especially when it comes to language patterns. Rapport is the frame in which you hang your sales. No rapport usually results in no sale and always results in no repeat or referral sales. Covert rapport, as the name suggests, is the variety of subtle and almost invisible ways which one can use to rapidly create and maintain rapport.

When it comes to language patterns, you should consciously mirror the way your buyer speaks. If they talk slowly, you also want to speak slowly, and if they speak quickly, follow suit. The same goes for whether they speak loudly or quietly. Tailor your speech to mirror that of the customer.

You will notice that quiet talkers do not connect easily to those who speak loudly. Although, loud talkers will tolerate a quiet talker. Still, matching is your best approach to increasing your bond with the prospective buyer. Also, the more you can observe tone and inflection, the more nuances you will notice in people. Essentially, you want to modulate your speech patterns to sound more like your customer.

I'm sure most of us have been on a vacation somewhere, and when we returned home found that we had picked up some of the mannerisms or accents of the people we had been around. This is an example of the natural, subconscious tendency we all have of mirroring people when trying to fit in.

Most people like themselves, so the more you act like them, the less resistance they will have for you.

Dressing for Success—Knowing Your Customer Base

Clothing is another important aspect of building rapport. Dress appropriately to your marketplace, your brand, your culture, to management requirements, and to your own personality. You may even want to give some thought to how your consistent clothing style might be modulated to become a part of your personal "schtick" or brand.

Another thing to keep in mind is that rural people generally dress a bit more casually, whereas people who live in the larger cities tend to be a little more dressed up.

The main point is that the buyer will have an expectation of you based on the market and brand you're selling and how they expect people to dress in your business.

One last thought regarding clothing is to dress in layers. Ideally, you should have both a dress jacket and also a casual jacket at work. That way, you can dress up or down on the spot by choice of jacket or no jacket at all, changing your clothing on the fly. If someone is very casual, and you're wearing a suit and tie or something a little bit more formal, don't be afraid to roll up your sleeves or undo your tie during the conversation. This technique works quite well to relax your customer. You can dress up or dress down while you work with a client to mirror their overall formality of dress or to send a signal as to where you are in the sale.

Duane Brain Tip

Reader, I will often change my body posture, roll my sleeves up or down, cap or uncap my pen, and tidy up or spread out papers during different points of the sale to indicate either a change in mood or where we are time-wise in the process.

Culture Wise is Sales Wise

Your office should also be comfortable for every type of personality who enters it. It should be a mirror image of your personality and market, but not a shrine. It should be presentable and comfortable to all races, religions, ages, demographics and sexual orientations. Don't keep anything in your office that would be offensive to anyone.

I love different cultures and have a lot of different cultural friends partly because I grew up on soccer fields. I was able to learn a lot about cultural selling through my own experience in dealing with many different cultures. Do a search on Google and YouTube to learn more about "cultural selling". You'll also find a great resource on Marino TV for this. When you have a chance, check out my "Cultural Selling" segments at www.DuaneMarino.com/marino-tv. This will give you additional insights into the subject.

While we're on the subject, I recently had my DNA tested and learned some surprising and interesting things about my ancestors. I'm mostly Italian/Croatian/Austrian, which wasn't a surprise. But, as it turns out, I also have a large portion of South American Colombian Indian and Mongolian DNA! Talk about a great conversation topic and way to bond with all sorts of people. So drop all your prejudices as anyone and everyone can be your ancestor or customer, and bear in mind that you may not know your own background as well as you think you do.

Don't neglect the little details, either. Even your pen makes a statement about who you are. It shouldn't be overdone, nor should it be understated. If you're using a gold, diamond-studded five-hundred dollar pen while selling an average-priced product to average people, it will convey the wrong message to your buyer. Don't risk coming across as arrogant or disingenuous or trying too hard to impress simply because you chose an inappropriate pen.

In life, perception is reality. Creating the right perception for a prospective buyer is at the very core of the art of sales. You need to understand your prospect's reality, and you need to be able to merge it with your own.

On the other hand, sporting a chewed-up, 59-cent plastic pen, particularly if you've got half your chicken sandwich still stuck on it after having used it as a toothpick, does not convey an image of professionalism, not to mention good hygiene. What you need is a good, standard, stainless-steel pen, without any logos (other than your brand). Even a logo can cause some people to think that you may be affiliated with different companies or suppliers, which could injure your cause in some sales scenarios.

When it comes to jewelry, less is more. Don't wear excessive or gaudy jewelry, although wearing some in moderation is fine, if it is part of your personality.

Avoid wearing colognes and perfumes. Although cleanliness is important, understand that some people are actually allergic to fragrant products. A particular fragrance may even remind them of something or someone that they don't like. Bear in mind that the stereotypical image of the cheesy salesman of the past is a loud and fast talker in a gaudy, plaid jacket who is overloaded with jewelry and heavy cologne. You don't want to feed into that with your own appearance. Err on the side of caution so you don't chance a sale by a mistake that could have been easily avoided in the first place.

I used to dislike tattoos and never understood why someone would get one, but when my father passed away, I felt strongly compelled to get three tattoos of different images that held special meaning for us. As important as these tattoos are to me, I still made sure to get them in discreet places so that I could choose when, or even if, I would show them to anyone. Be aware of the fact that customers and employers will judge a book by its cover, so be mindful of what you put on *your* cover!

Overt Rapport

Overt rapport is a study of the more obvious and observable ways we can build rapport by matching things such as common interests and personal values.

If the buyer likes to play golf, then show some interest in golf, even if you don't play it. "Oh, wow! I'd love to play! Where do you usually play? What a great way to get some time in the fresh air!"

While it's fine to wax enthusiastic about your customer's interests, it's never wise to act like you know something about subjects you don't really understand. Lying about anything opens you up to the possibility of getting caught on it. If a prospect finds you lying about a little thing, chances are he won't trust you with the bigger things. It can be lethal to a sale and will cost you a prospect's trust. Lies are difficult to keep track of. It's very difficult to have a memory that good. Also, people know when you're faking it. For one thing, there is always a particular lingo in any field, and using the wrong terminology is a dead giveaway. The moment a lie is detected, you're toast, and you can kiss your sale, the referrals and the repeats goodbye. Continue to do it, and it will eventually deteriorate your reputation. Show common interest in them and what they value without lying or stretching the truth about what you know.

Words create thoughts, and thoughts cause feelings, the magnitude of which will lead to action or inaction.

When you're being genuine, there's no need to tread cautiously with the need to choose your words carefully. Simply be honest and sincere. People will like and respect you for it, and they will want to buy from you and only you.

Handshake Language

The way we shake someone's hand also says a lot about us. Handshakes are another way of communicating. Different types of handshakes convey different messages. Shaking with one hand outright in a straight, up and down motion communicates something entirely different than placing your hand on top or underneath. A double-clutch hand-shake, where you take hold of the back of a person's hand while you shake, is a different type of handshake altogether.

Handshakes such as: touching someone's forearm or upper arm; gently guiding their shoulder with your other arm as you turn toward where you want to go; and correcting a loose grip or missed grip as a bit of a joke while handshak-ing all show you are confident and fun. Complimenting the person on his strong grip right after he almost breaks your hand can also be fun and helps to reset control.

You might sense that some people don't want to shake hands, and that's fine too. There could be cultural reasons for this, or perhaps they are germophobic.

You can see that handshakes are another useful and elegant way to communicate who you are as a person before or after the sale.

Regarding your words, again, it's not so much what you say, but how you say it. For example, depending on the tone of your voice, the word "no" can have dozens of meanings. You could ask it as a question or say it as a statement. You could sound frustrated, curious or shocked. You could say "no" as if something were funny, as if you were relieved, or you could say it to show that you actually mean the opposite.

It is not so much the words themselves as it is the way you say things—the inflection, mood, meaning and intention behind the words. A great exercise right now would be to try to say the word "no" with as many different meanings as possible just by changing your tone, body language and facial expressions.

Eye on Communication

Then, of course, there is the use of your eyes. It has been said that the eyes are the windows to the soul. People will pick up your mood, your intentions and your emotional state from your eyes.

Duane Brain Tip

Reader, commit to looking into your buyer's right eye, which, of course, is on your left side. When you look into someone's right eye, your abilities to be present and communicate effectively are far greater than going back and forth between their eyes or even looking at their left eye. This is something that has to be experienced to really believe and appreciate, so try it for yourself. If you're curious as to why this works, send me an email, and I will be happy to explain it.

A proper amount of eye contact is important. In a normal conversation, average eye contact is probably about two-thirds of the conversation. If you look at them too much, it could be perceived as a bit aggressive or creepy. There are some cultures, such as the Portuguese, that consider a lot of eye contact a sign of respect, whereas other cultures

and people (such as Asians who grew up in large population centers) consider excessive eye contact a sign of bad
manners or aggression. As a general rule, maintaining eye
contact for about two-thirds of a conversation is regarded
as a comfortable range for most people.

A lot can be gained by observing someone's eyes and
matching their general tone. For example, tired people are
often turned off by perky people. If you ever see a customer
walk up to a receptionist looking awfully tired as they ask
for a salesperson, just walk up and act a little tired yourself
for the first couple of minutes. Being too energetic will put
them off and irritate them, because they just don't feel up
to it. Remember, you want them to become your customer.
Once you match them, then you can pace and lead them
into a more energetic mood. You can't lead someone you
haven't matched and paced as it will result in an instant
breakdown in rapport and stuck communications.

Power Profiling

As mentioned earlier, bumper stickers, mirror danglers,
the things hanging from their key chains, and the comments on their t-shirts are all great ways of understanding
personality types. These kinds of things can guide you in
knowing what to talk about and what subjects to avoid.
Cell phones and watches can be great conversational items.

"I love your watch! Where did you get it?"

"How do you like your new phone? I'm thinking about
changing brands."

"How do you live without a watch?"

"How do you live without a cell phone?"

"These shouldn't even be called cell phones anymore because most people avoid using the phone! How do you use yours the most?"

Such conversation starters are powerful ways to quickly profile people and get them talking about themselves. Most people love to talk about themselves.

Last but not least is the art of building better relationships by being a good listener. Being a good listener is pure gold. You may find people telling you things like, "I don't know what it is about you, but I really enjoy my time with you. You're such a good friend." What they probably mean is that you don't talk too much and that you're a great listener. From this, we learn that there are two simple words you should never forget in sales, and they are simply, "Be quiet." Or, if needed, "Shut up."

We're certainly not learning anything if we're always talking. You will collect a lot more information if you allow the other person to talk. For this reason, after you ask a reasonable question, be quiet. Wait one or two seconds after their reply before you ask your next question, to make sure the person has completed their train of thought.

Actively listening, paying attention to your buyer, becoming them, and matching their communication style are all skills that will go a long way in generating a strong rapport with your buyers and a lot of sales throughout your career.

Sales Language

Let's have a look at the power of communication as it relates to language and how we need to be sensitive about and perhaps update our sales language.

If you've ever seen a 1940's black-and-white movie, what

you'll find is that although the actors are speaking English, the language has changed drastically since then. If you were to speak today like they did in the '40s, people around you would think you had lost your mind. Communicating differently from others causes discomfort.

Because sales is hundreds of years old, and the car business is over a century old, there is a lot of outdated language still used in this business. Things are very different nowadays than when this industry started—profits were larger, people's buying habits have changed significantly, and even attitudes towards female buyers vs. male buyers have shifted drastically. Because this business is old, some of the language is old and can be stale and downright inappropriate for today's market.

Part of the problem of using old sales language is that the answers you elicit from your prospects will be as rote and tired as the language you use. If your buyer has heard the same language before from previous salespeople in your industry, he will be "trained" to respond with the same answers he's given in the past without giving any real thought to them. If you ask stupid questions, you get stupid answers. Once you get false or bad information, you've missed your opportunity, and you will have that much more resistance to overcome later in the sale. The right choice of words gets the job done much more efficiently while also avoiding the pitfalls of using the wrong language and potentially offending your customer.

Below is a chart that compares the old and "dangerous" industry language to my modern, and safer, sales language. Practice your new vocabulary by going up and down the list three times and reading each column, line by line.

As you go through for the first time, compare the two columns. Notice that you can get the same job done in a much less confrontational way, and probably elicit a lot more quality information from the buyer if you use the phrases on the right side of the page.

Next, fold the page over or cover the left column with your hand, and come down the right column, reading it out loud.

On your third pass through, read just the right column again. This time, adjust your tone and body language to match how it would be in a real-life situation, and imagine where in the sales process it would typically come up as well as when and how it could be used.

Creates Resistance	Creates FLOW
Are you buying today?	When could we have your car?
Are you buying today?	Delivery could be as soon as…?
Any other decision makers?	Is anyone else driving or helping with selection, pricing or paperwork?
The List/Sticker/MSRP (Manufacturer's Suggested Retail Price) is….	It's built to sell for $… (BTSF)
We're asking….	It's priced to sell for $… (PTSF)
The next up is mine.	I'm on deck; I'll greet this guest.
You're upside down.	You're currently in a rather awkward trading position.
Could I have a deposit?	With transactions like these, do you normally hold or secure them with a credit card, cash, or debit?

What can you afford?	Any thoughts on the numbers?
This is the contract/bill of sale.	This is the paperwork.
Let me tell/explain this to you.	Here's a thought, let me share….
We'll call our wholesalers.	We call our outside buyers and get bids.
We do an appraisal.	We do a market assessment/review.
What color do you want?	Is there a color we must avoid? Do you have a 2nd or 3rd favorite?
Let's work out a deal.	Let's come to an agreement.

What would it take for me to earn your business?	What conditions need to be met before we can move forward?
If I could, would you…?	If we came to an arrangement, agreement or accommodation on that, delivery could be as soon as….
Do you have a trade?	Would this be an addition or replacement for your car?
What do you want for your trade?	Has it been professionally assessed recently, and did you finance it?
That offer is below invoice.	As a reseller, we also have some fixed costs of….
It's loaded/It's base.	Fully Equipped/Nicely Equipped.
We'll do a locate/dealer trade.	We'll check regional pool stock.
I need your signature and credit card to show my manager you're committed.	A quick OK with some security, and I'll see if management will agree to your offer.

(If you have any questions about this chart, please send me an email, and I will be happy to respond.)

"Sales are made or lost by a few words, not a few dollars."

—*Tom Hopkins*

Rest assured, I can tell you from hundreds of my own sales experiences, and from those of thousands of my sales students, that the questions and statements in the right-hand column are of much better quality and are much less offensive to many demographics and individuals of all ages.

When you try them out in your sales processes, you're going to find out for yourself that some work almost like magic. Give some serious thought to changing your language and the way you speak.

Here's the thing with language: when you change the way you talk, you change the way you think. When you change the way you talk to your buyer, you change the way he/she thinks about you and the whole situation. If you want better results, change your language.

Remember, you are the master of your unspoken words. Once spoken, they are the master of you.

The Difference Between Public and Private Information

It should also be pointed out that there is a difference between what I call public and private information. Some of the information that we, as sales professionals, are going for early in the sale today is what I refer to as private information.

"Normal" individuals with good credit generally don't respond well to private probing questions and information when asked too early in the sales process. They'll mislead you with their answers to protect themselves and their interests because they can. If you've ever heard the phrase, "Buyers are liars," some of the reality of this is that we, as salespeople, are responsible for creating this by asking inappropriate, aggressive or private questions prematurely, which forces them to become defensive and lie.

Public Questions

A public question is one that doesn't make someone feel uncomfortable answering or lying to you about. Public questions don't cause them to feel like there is any need to protect themselves or to exaggerate their own position. The usage of private vs. public questions is mostly about timing.

Private Questions

Typical private information that we sometimes try to obtain too early from some of our customers are things like budget, decision-makers, and time-frames.

Generally, the only people who are going to give you an honest budget, let you know who the decision-maker really is, or give you the correct time-frame early in the sale—before you've established a good connection and sufficient credibility—are people who are not quite mentally or emotionally stable, or somebody with bad credit.

If you meet someone who immediately starts telling you all about themselves—too much and too quickly—he or she is probably not very stable, may have questionable credit, and you should consider this a yellow or red flag.

I recommend that you read the questions listed above and determine the best times in your sales process to ask them to help you build an ideal sales puzzle with your prospective buyers. See how you can get better information by asking better questions at the appropriate points in your process. Ask reasonable questions at reasonable times.

A few of "the old" questions will negatively affect your gross profit or give people the wrong impression of what you are doing in the sales process. A couple of them will take you out of stock, and a few will actually be demeaning to the product or product line or even insult your customer.

So, in the name of improvement, take a sensitive look at your language of sales, and bring back some proper bedside manners where they might be needed. Ask yourself how you would feel if a salesperson asked *you* these questions. Revisit the entire concept of sales language and see the difference it can make to your closing ratios and income.

CHAPTER 10

Power #3: Your Power of Relationships

The Pareto Principle, or 80/20 rule, states that you get the majority (about 80%) of your repeats and referrals from the minority (about 20%) of your customers. Once you isolate your most effective strategies and ideal clients, you can start to apply them to your selling day and your customer base. And, over time, you will find that your best customers will indeed send you the majority of your repeat and referral business. When this starts to happen, you've gained the momentum you need to really start reaping the fruits of your labor!

Most of us are aware of the fact that our own mindset significantly affects how well things turn out, but what else separates our sales levels and determines our current and future earning potential? Selling is in fact very similar to fishing. There are really only three ways we can fish and three ways we can sell:

- Waiting
- Pursuing
- Attracting

Waiting for Customers
(Level One Selling)

Let's go with the fishing analogy and then tie it right back into selling. Our first way of selling (or what I call "Level One Selling") is done by waiting. If all you do is wait for a fish (or customers) to jump on the line, you might be able to survive and keep your JOB (as in, "Just Over Broke"). This type of scenario offers a life of juggling bills, living off of credit cards, and other "living on the brink" scenarios. Not to mention long, stressful hours hanging around, hoping and praying the right person walks in when you're available or when it's your turn in the rotation to take traffic.

Picture going down to a river with a fishing rod, casting your line and lure into the water and sitting back to wait for a bite, with 10 other people all doing the same thing within 30 feet of you.

In a recreational setting, it can be quite relaxing while having an afternoon off. But if your family relies on your catch as their sole source of food, and you continue to sit back and relax while waiting for something to take your bait with 10 other people all fishing from the same hole, and if this does not produce any catches worth mentioning for a couple days—or weeks—you are going to run into difficulty.

Imagine coming home empty-handed day after day, and your son or daughter asks you, "Papa, how was your day? Did you catch us some dinner?" And so you tell them, after mustering up some strength, "Great! I didn't catch any fish, but I thought I had one for a moment. It was my rod and reel's fault, of course, not mine. But there's always tomorrow, right?"

Your kids might ask you, "Where did you go?" And you tell

them you went to the same place you've been going for the past few days.

Even your kids will have the sense to ask you, "Why don't you try something different or change things up a bit? Try a different lure. Switch to a worm. Try a different hook. Try a different part of the river. Wade in. Go to a different depth or distance from shore. Try new things, Papa!"

"Never giving up" can sometimes be bad advice, especially if you equate that with never trying anything new or different. A salesperson is by nature a hopeful and optimistic creature. There's always a slight sense of morale kept simply for the fact that we're at least working and have a place to go to in the morning. But I have also seen salespeople who have relied for years almost entirely on Level One Selling—waiting—who became bitter and very negative towards the world.

If you were to go to a bring-your-kids-to-work day, would you be yourself, acting like you normally do? Or would you have to fake it a little? Would you be embarrassed of how you behave and spend your time at work?

The answer to that question actually tells us a lot about our conscience as it relates to our work. How hard *do* you actually try to make things happen for yourself? Most importantly, how well *are* you doing?

If you brought your child to work with you, what might you do differently than what you normally do? It's a valid question that might give you a moment of pause and a different point of view to assess your professional life from.

Doing little more than waiting for walk-ins, phone calls or emails are three predominant ways that many salespeople currently "survive" in this business. When it's quiet, they hang out in the huddle. But take a look at the math of this type of traffic in today's business. In an average month, most stores or dealerships will get about twenty to twenty-five opportunities per salesperson from fresh traffic—about one per day. Based on the industry norm's closing ratio of about 1 of 4, you are looking at only about four to six sales in a month! An honest look at these numbers clearly shows the need to do more than just wait for traffic.

Maybe it's time to start changing it up and begin pursuing the fish. This change in strategy always starts with a change in your own psychology: first you have to recognize that what you are doing is not producing the results you want.

My father always told me that if you are not getting the results you want, it's either your information, your execution, or both.

There are many different ways you can pursue your customers.

Pursuing Customers
(Level Two Selling)

Going after your customers requires changing how you sell. You have to have the confidence to step out of your comfort zone and mix things up a bit, try new things. To do this, you need to study your craft and be continually on the lookout for new ways to connect with people.

There are many different ways you can pursue your customers. You can do this by using a telephone, going on Facebook, using your company's database, even going to public places such as a restaurant or festival. People are everywhere. Why wait for a small handful to call, email or stumble in? Reach out! Find someone to talk to. Create interest in you and what you have. If you do this, you will never be without a prospective buyer.

Let's take a look at the difference. Your company generates the phone, Internet, email and walk-in traffic because of its physical location, reputation, brands it sells and the advertising it does. And you will close a certain percentage of the traffic generated. You probably work on a strict rotation honor system or open floor, but, from my viewpoint, all those leads should be seen as a gift from your company rather than relied upon as your sole supply. They are a privilege and not a right as you should only have access to that traffic if you adhere to your company's sales processes, activities and expected results.

To move from a job to a career, you will need to add the people you pursue to all that "free bonus" traffic that walks in. Some of these people will become prospects, and a few will turn into sales. The result will be more sales, a better income, more independence, and less stress. A good rule of thumb is that, in any given month, you can expect to close about the same number of warm leads that you develop on average per day. So, three warm leads developed per day, every day, on average, will result in about three additional sales per month.

I have almost seventy modern and effective strategies for pursuing business besides waiting for walk-in traffic, but it would require a book on its own just to document them all. However, you can access them instantly on MarinoTV online. Just contact our office for a subscription.

When I train on-site at my clients' dealerships, I take traffic and make phone calls live, in front of the entire team. I love it when the sales team randomly hands me the names and numbers of people to contact. At a large Chrysler dealership in Toronto (population 5 million), a salesperson handed me some service customers to call from a huge list. I called half a dozen and booked a couple of appointments. One was to a cell phone for a customer named Frank, and I booked him in to look at the new Dodge Challenger. Later that day, a different salesperson randomly opened the Yellow Pages (which in Toronto is about 3 inches thick) and dropped his finger on a random number, which I then called using my "Random 10 Second Survey Business Prospecting" word track.

The person answering the phone said the one thing I wasn't prepared to hear: "Duane, this is Frank. We spoke this morning, and I'm already coming in to see you about a new Challenger!"

It took us all a few seconds to register! What are the chances of a random selection from a service list, and then calling that same person again by random selection from a phone book in a city with over 5 million residents! My sales friends, you and I have had things like this happen dozens of times. It seems to prove that in some strange way, we are all connected!

If you would like some help working your customer base using the phone, we have our own call center—a BDC for hire called TNT—and it really is dynamite! We can help you make your month! We happily make a large quantity of quality contacts using customized powerful proprietary word tracks to book sales appointments. We will also pass on leads to you of people who will be in the market soon, identify customers who want to buy but think they are credit challenged, and uncover customer complaints. Feel free to call us at 1-888-735-6275, visit www.DuaneMarino.com, or email us at info@duanemarino.com for a free quote.

Attracting Customers
(Level Three Selling)

Let's step up our game one more level and discuss how any salesperson can literally make money while they sleep. Let's go back to our fishing analogy for a moment. Picture a fisherman going down to the water's edge and throwing some corn into the water. By giving the fish something they want, the fish that were previously nowhere to be found now quickly come up to him. Our fisherman has gone from waiting to pursuing, and now attracting fish.

Likewise, you want to attract customers—not just wait for them to randomly show up or spend all your time pursuing them. This can be done in many ways, but by becoming their "friend in the car business", (or whatever business you are in) people will start asking for you, and this will result in crucial repeats and referrals. By creating this association and positioning yourself as their "go to" person and an industry expert, you will go far beyond being merely a "salesperson" who sells products; you will be exponentially more productive.

When people who have met you think of your product, they should also think of you—a non-severable association (a bond) between your product and you—with a lot of positive feelings for both. As a matter of fact, anytime they have a question about a product you sell, you should be the first person they call for answers, assistance and purchases. Ideally, this should happen a lot for you. If they see you as their trusted friend in the business, they will call you first and give you a shot at their business.

You want to grow your loyal customer base until you can make your living off of that power base alone. And as you start attracting even more customers, it becomes easier and easier to do it more and more. Nowadays, it is much easier to create a network of raving fans than ever before, thanks to the Internet. When you start to attract customers, you will create a lifestyle. Let's look at the math of this. We've gone over walk-in sales—closing around a quarter of the people you meet. Next, we went over pursuing prospects, knowing that we will close about the same number of warm prospects per month as we develop per day.

Now we are going to look at something called Critical Mass Numbers. These numbers are the ratios you need to understand in order to reduce your dependency on lot traffic and to really start attracting the kind of business you need to thrive, and not just survive. Here's a really good guide:

Let's pretend you had a hundred friends who had first-point association with you for a product you are selling. First-point association is what your friends associate you with initially when they think of you. In other words, when those hundred people who know you think of you, they think of what you sell, and when they think of what you sell, they think of you. They might also know you in other ways in life, but when they think of you, their first point of association is with your product. The goal is to make this true for all of your customers, all of your networks and all of your connections.

If there were a hundred people with whom you had this first-point association, about a fifth of them would generate new business for you via referrals and repeats every year. We are talking about a hundred friends who think of you as their "friend in the car business," not just a hundred people you've simply sold something to or people you know. It's likely you have a hundred Facebook friends, but do all of those people think of you first when they think of needing or wanting what you sell? Probably not—at least not yet.

If you can generate twenty sales a year from a hundred people who think of you as their "friend in the car business," then two hundred people will give you forty sales; three hundred people draw in sixty sales, and so on. It can add up quickly. This is Level Three selling—attracting customers.

If you want to sell a hundred units in a year to nothing but your own client base through nothing but attraction, you need about five hundred people who instantly and effortlessly think of you as their friend in that business.

In reality, your sales will be a combination of Level One (waiting), Level Two (pursuing) and Level Three (attracting) for most of us. This pattern actually holds true across all different industries, whether it's real estate, insurance, or something else entirely.

The average to below-average salesperson gets most of their business from Level One (waiting), a little bit from Level Two (pursuing), and very little from Level Three (attracting). Angels acquire most of their sales from Level Three, a little from Level Two, and they never rely on Level One. They are angelic because they have gotten themselves to a point where they can independently generate their own prospects, customers, and sales.

If you effectively manage all three types of sales leads— attraction, pursuit, and waiting—every day, on and off the job; and if you are organized, have good sales energy, and keep your head and heart in the game, you can make a fortune in this business and probably any other sales industry as well. I can list out hundreds of people I've met who have done exactly that, including myself. If my business had to rely on fresh traffic, I would have burned out and cashed out a long time ago.

Remember, you can't close an empty chair, and you can't

sell a secret. So, if no one knows a thing about you or has never heard of you, you have a huge challenge ahead of yourself. But you have to start somewhere. You have to sell yourself first and keep reselling yourself to your community and clients.

Duane Brain Tip

Reader, imagine how you would feel if you bought a couch, and your sales and service rep's idea of a "follow-up" was something like this:

"Is Dooaney Marineow there?" (Not pronouncing your name properly.)

"Do you know anybody looking for a couch?"

"We are having a sale this weekend on couches." (This call continues every three months forever.)

"How many couches are in your household? How many sitters? Who is probably next in line for a new couch?"

"New couches are very complicated. The nicest used ones go the quickest. Give me your friend's number, and I will call them."

"It's time to clean your couch and tighten its legs again!" (This call also continues every three months into eternity.)

After how many of these types of calls would you stop picking up the phone or stop calling them back? Two? Three? Your business may be flatlining or declining due to well-intended but excessive—and downright stupid—after-sale contacts. I remember the days before we had Call Display or Caller ID, when everyone would rush to the house phone out of curiosity. Even if we shut our ringers off, the flashing red light usually got the best of us, and we'd pick up the phone. But this was a long time ago. Most of the techniques I just shared were created in the 1950s B.G. and long before Call Display. I know for a fact some out-of-touch training companies and old school trainers still teach that garbage.

In the next chapter, we will take a look at how to develop memorable and favorable relationships, which will help with the third level of attracting customers.

Becoming Favorably Memorable

We have all experienced calling a customer and having them answer the first time, but then are unable to reach them after that. Most likely, they saw on their Caller ID that it was you, and, since they thought that you were not valuable to them on the last call, they decided not to answer or call back on the next one. Worse yet, if the last contact was not enjoyable for them, and the call seemed as if it was only valuable for you, they may never pick up the phone again. You know you screen your calls with your Call Display or Caller ID, and so do your customers. This little piece of technology has changed our sales world. Have you really thought this through yet?

No matter what business you are in, the point of being favorably memorable and valuable after delivery, as well as becoming the customer's friend, is so that you can simultaneously reduce your stress, increase your appointments, raise your sales and explode your income at some near point in your future through repeats and referrals. This will happen once you start to create real relationships with your customers and not just fake it through "follow-ups".

But how do we, as salespeople, build powerful and authentic relationships that ensure we are remembered by our customers?

For one thing, forget the old style, lifeless client scripts that most training manuals request you use in your phone calls every few months to get referrals. Your customers are wise to that and won't respond. I understand CRM very well. As I've said, I launched the very first Windows-based CRM piece in the automotive business, complete with scripts and call schedules. Well, our customers are onto us now.

Instead of that being your only game plan, you can start by showing up every day with the energy, conviction and love of your business and customers that has been described earlier. By doing what the customer doesn't expect regarding great customer service, and by doing what other salespeople don't do in going the extra mile for customers, you will immediately position yourself above the average in their minds and hearts. And even if you are but 1% above average in your work ethic, attitude and processes, you are eventually going to get above average results. I love sales and being self-employed because I get out what I put in.

Remember, success comes from hard work. Most people simply give up before they see results. The ability to remain on a course and push through opposition is a prerequisite to success, in any area of life. Just keep showing up until everyone else gives up.

Here are some more tips on how to be enjoyable and valuable to your clients after the sale, and this is how you will become favorably memorable with your best clients. Evaluate these with your head, heart and gut, and then start doing what makes sense to you:

1. Don't Lie

If you lie, people will remember you in the wrong way. I read somewhere that if someone is happy, they'll tell a couple of people. If they're not, they'll tell ten. Who knows the real number? The point is, we know that an upset customer can cause a lot of damage. In this day and age, because of technology and social media, people can push your name the wrong way. As I've said a long slow death through negativity on social media is the ultimate price one can pay. All of our markets are too small, and the Internet is too big, to get away with lying. As they say, the truth will set you free, and it has never been truer since the creation of the Internet.

2. Don't Move to Work for a Different Company or Change Locations

As a salesperson, the moment you change dealerships or companies, you'll lose your connections with all those people and some credibility. Most of them won't follow you to your new location; you are very much a package deal. They like you at that location, selling that brand, connected to that service department. As soon as that formula changes, the vast majority of your clients will absolutely not follow you to the next store.

Deciding to retire at the store you're at right now could be one of the best things you do for your stress levels and income down the road. By default, you'll probably become one of the top salespeople simply because you'll become part of the furniture.

It is true that management does change, and sometimes the owners will. I've even seen the brands change, but that top salesperson does not leave their piece of pavement or that desk for any of those reasons. Stay put.

3. Adopt a "Can do!" Attitude

You definitely want this kind of mindset when someone calls on you: "I can do that," "I can handle that," "I'm on it," "Leave it to me," and, "I'll get back to you quickly, thanks for calling me." Don't pass the buck to someone else. Be the guy or gal who wants to do something for their client.

4. Stand Out and Be Remembered

Create a schtick. A schtick is a particular trait or characteristic that a person can be remembered by simply because of its "standout factor" or uniqueness. It can be as simple as wearing a hat or scarf when everyone else in the sales force does not. I shaved my head way back in 1996. I remember this because my daughter was four years old, and it was the year before I ventured off into my own training business. A schtick is a way of acting, behaving or looking. So, in the name of having a schtick, I shaved my head inspired by Patrick Stewart's look in Star Trek at the time. I thought I could probably pull that off. I've never tried to grow it back in, and I have no idea what I would have left if I tried to, but I use my shaved head to my advantage.

My promoter John Kostakos' mentor is Bob Mohr, the world's most prolific speaker promoter. John and Bob referred Joe Girard to me. It was also Bob's advice years ago to make my face my logo, and he told me to put it on everything I create. People sometimes remember me as "the trainer with the shaved head" or occasionally call me Dan Marino. Just by pure luck, my name sounds like Dan Marino, the great NFL football quarterback for the Miami Dolphins. Positive association has never hurt anyone either. Being memorable as a salesperson, being unique, likable and familiar, are powerful bond-building elements.

Other things that could be unique are your office, something on your desk, your body size and frame, your personality, a nickname, something about your background, your accent, or some maxim or saying that you say often. The possibilities are endless. The secret is to hold on to it and not change it. The power of this is in the consistency. Obviously, it should also be something positive or neutral—not something repulsive in its nature.

Anything that you leverage and make consistently unique and noticeable becomes your anchor and your schtick.

5. Have Your Picture on Your Business Card

Having your picture on your business card is something I believe in immensely. I know there are some brands, companies and dealerships that don't advocate that, but I believe that is poor psychology.

Many customers buy where they buy because of the salesperson. By having your picture on your business card, you are more memorable after the sale because we are built to remember faces, not names.

If you are more memorable and easier to find after delivery, it means more sales for the company and manufacturer.

I'm a strong supporter of having your picture on your business card and everything else you send out as well, but make sure you update your picture annually!

6. Create a Professional and Consistent Marketplace Image in Social Media

In addition to the emails you send out, it's worthwhile to have professional-looking social media accounts such as Facebook, Twitter, LinkedIn, and your YouTube channel (you can have two or three of each of these if you'd like).

This helps to improve your image, your network with your clients, and to become consistent and professional in the marketplace.

On these accounts, you would regularly blast out a tip, a quote or a post—like a cute bumper sticker, pictures of your customers picking up their new SUVs, or even a recipe. But the name of the game is to be accessible on all social media. Have a presence for all to see, and be active with your posts.

Keep in mind that you want to be long on value, quirkiness and fun, and very short on promotion, sales and deals. That way, people won't take you off their list or just associate you with pushing product since they are getting a lot of value and enjoyment from it. Then, once in a while, mention your sale or promotion. Just make sure the majority of your posts are related to your industry.

All major promotions should come from the company or the manufacturer, not the salesperson. The salesperson sells love, themselves, relationships; the straightforward promoting comes from the manufacturer or the company.

When the company's promotion reaches your client who knows you and has a great sales relationship with you—because everything you did after the sale was enjoyable and valuable for them—you will get the inquiries and sales for those repeats and referrals.

7. Offer a Service Valet

This is not only for selling cars in particular; this can apply to selling other products as well. Call and offer a random service pick-up.

Watch the service database daily, and if you notice that you have a great customer coming in for service, you can call them up and say, "Hello, Mrs. Customer! I noticed you're coming in for service on Thursday. I'd like to pick up your car and drop it off when it's done. It's probably warranty work, so there is no charge anyway. If there is, we can reconcile everything after the fact. I'll leave you a car for the day, and we can coordinate the drop-off or pick-up later on in the day as things get wrapped up."

This will give you a lot of good rapport with that individual because they know it is above and beyond the call of duty and nobody else does this kind of thing. Additionally, everybody that day is going to ask your customer, "What's with the new car?" and they are going to have to mention your name in a very favorable way.

What a wonderful way to network with all of your clients' friends and families, just by doing one random service pick-up!

If you live in a town or marketplace outside of where your dealer sells, then I highly recommend you tell everyone in your community that your dealer picks up and drops off vehicles for service. You become the local support for your out-of-town employer.

Do this with love, and you will own your town. Your sales will be very high in the marketplace where you live if they know that you're a person in the local town who is actually their friend in the car business that services them in this way.

8. Make it Easy for Them to Reach You

When you sell your product, you can probably attach a sticker with your name and phone number to it, or place the sticker in the owner's manual in case they need a repair or some technical assistance.

In automotive, you can make sure your customers are comfortable with the technology in their vehicles when they get their cars by showing them how to use the interactive electronic devices now available. At the same time, you can program your cell phone number or your dealership's service number in their address book during the Bluetooth setup. It will be right there when they need it.

Duane Brain Tip

When doing the vehicle delivery orientation, get permission to sync the customer's phone for them. Be sure to warn them that any calls or messages that come in may be displayed or played in the car for all to hear and see! I have been witness to some very awkward situations that could have been avoided. Yikes!

Offer your help. Don't just transfer the call when a client calls with questions or issues. It is so common for salespeople to have zero interest in someone once the sale has been completed. Not only is this selfish, heartless and wrong on many levels in how people should act towards one another, just think of the power you have when you're their guy or gal who is concerned and cares! Don't even think of transferring the phone call before doing everything you can to help or offer support.

For example, if a customer you sold a car to calls to let you know that she's been in an accident, your first response should be, "That's terrible! Are you okay?" The next thing you do is let them know they're in good hands with you. "Let me coordinate with the body shop for you. Where can I get back to you regarding what we can do?" You do not just transfer them to another department because that is really a blow off. You're kind of saying that this is not your problem. "I'm not the guy to deal with regarding your problem. I only sold you the car. That's not what I do. That's not my department."

If you are not helping your customers after the sale—if you are not in the customer service business after delivery—then you might as well understand that when you transfer that call, you are also transferring all the referrals and repeat business to your competitor. The same goes for anything you might sell. The person has a question about the item, answer it and be of service to them. At the very least, quarterback the concern or complaint until it is easily and properly passed off to the appropriate person or department. They called you because they already like, respect and remember you, and they need your help.

9. Know Other People in Your Business

Be connected with people at other companies within your industry. For example, if you sell cars, establish friendships with people who work in related industries, such as car washes, independent tire shops, auto parts stores, insurance people, and any outside supplier. You want to have friends in the business you are in so that you can leverage these contacts amongst other people and cross refer customers within that network.

10. Contact Your Customers on Their Birthdays.

Whether you do it by text message, email, a phone call, or a mail-out card, send your customers a birthday greeting. You can probably coordinate all of this information in your CRM or with your phone, or whatever database you're using. The idea is that you definitely want to contact people on their birthdays, and the information you need to do that is available to most of you. Someplace in your initial contractual agreement, customer's ID, or somewhere in the service records or sales records, you will usually have the customer's birthday. If not, make asking customers their birthdays a part of all your conversations, and make a note of it. It's a great way to let them know you're thinking of them and to remind them of you as well.

11. Keep Notes

You also want to keep and update your notes after every contact. These notes can be of their family, their occupation, their recreation, if they are taking a vacation, if somebody has passed away, or if they've had a baby. You want to refer to all of your notes every time before you pick up a call, so you don't put your foot in your mouth and reconnect with them seamlessly.

As a bonus, you can reference information from other calls to really make the customer feel that they are valuable and memorable to you. They will reciprocate by making you their "car guy" or "car gal". "So, how did your camping trip go a few months ago?" will make your customer feel important and make you feel like their friend.

12. Know Who is Calling You

Never proceed with a call if you don't recognize who it is that is calling. Get their last name or phone number, and call them back or put them on hold before you engage.

Then pull them up in your database or that of the company, or Google their name. Your customer obviously knows you because they called you! But if you don't recognize who they are well into a call, it could become very awkward and uncomfortable for both of you. And for them, the love affair with you could be over.

13. Remove the Nightmares

You will regret selling to some people, so remove the "nightmares", and get management approval to do so. There are some people who are not balanced psychologically, and they will cost you an excessive amount of time, energy, and effort after the sale.

No matter what the issue is, some people are just very difficult to get along with, and you are never going to get any traction with them or turn them around. They end up being a complete waste of time, and they drain you emotionally and maybe even financially. When it comes to such people, the best policy is "out of sight, out of mind". You want to get rid of the nightmares. Stop kidding yourself, talk to management, and remove them from your relationship marketing database.

Customer Relationship Marketing With Your Smartphone

A good way to develop and maintain customer relationships is through use of a CRM (software for Customer Relationship Management). Many businesses have such a program and database to keep track of all customers and leads. Used correctly, a CRM is a very useful tool.

However, one of the most powerful CRM tools ever developed is your smartphone. I've talked a lot about our "mobile computers that we can talk into" already. If you make good use of it, you can turn your smartphone into a highly effective Customer Relationship Management tool. Not only can it change the outcome of your business, but what's really great about it is that you carry it in your pocket or purse—and so do your buyers!

Once you've developed a network of people through your smartphone who also have you listed as one of their contacts, you will have truly generated a network of people who can send you more business. They can readily contact you directly and instantly 24/7, 365 days of the year from anywhere on the planet.

For example, if you happen to get a message from somebody on Sunday night at 11:30, they probably don't expect you to handle it right then. But they would like to know that you, their friend who sells for that company, received their message. In such a case, all they would really expect from you is a short note back that says, "Hi, I got your message. I'll get back to you first thing in the morning when I'm in the office."

Using your smartphone properly can push competitors completely out of the picture simply because of your accessibility. We are all lazy, so make it easy on your customers to reach you. It is human nature to take the path of least resistance. If your customers already love you and like dealing with you, they will not hesitate to call on you instead of spending time searching for someone else.

Here are some tips for making great use of your smartphone as a CRM tool:

- If you are in automotive sales, you can bring it into your appraisal process. You can use it to take photos of the trade-in, the VIN numbers, and the odometer.

- Permission-based photos of documentation instead of photocopies can really speed up the sale.

- Put your full customer's profile in your phone: what they do for a living, their childrens' names, their spouse's name, and update the info when things change because then you've got it right there in your phone. All smartphones have places for this information right in the contact manager.

- Keep ongoing notes in your phone. Any time you communicate with them, keep a short note about it. That way, the next time you contact them, you can go through the notes and refresh yourself with the data just as you would with the company's full-blown CRM.

- Most major company CRMs are now also compatible with mobile devices. If you have that, that's great. If not, use your phone as your personal CRM.

- Smartphones and the Internet are two big advantages that salespeople and customers have now compared to twenty or thirty years ago, when I first started in this business. Not fully embracing and utilizing this technology can put you at a considerable competitive disadvantage. However, I do know of some great salespeople who do not have cell or smartphones and practically live off the grid. In this day and age, that is so unusual. They use it as their schtick because not having a mobile phone is memorable!

- Another great use of your smartphone is to take a picture of the happy buyer when you deliver the product. Get the buyer's permission, and then take a picture of the two of you beside their brand-new purchase. If you are in real estate, take a picture of the buyer in front of the new house. If you're in car sales, take a photo of you and your buyer beside the car they bought with your dealership's name in the background. Then ask them if you can text or email them the picture on the spot.

Another great use of your smartphone is to take a picture of the happy buyer when you deliver the product.

- Also use this opportunity to ask them if they are on Facebook and other social media, and encourage them to tag your name there if they post the photo. You can also get their permission to post that picture on your own Facebook page and social media, and tag them.

- This is how you start getting connected with each other's family and friends instantly and for free. Remember also to save that picture as their contact photo on your phone so you also have that visual information every time their name comes up in your address book or when you contact each other.

- When it comes to reminders, you can place them all on your smartphone. If you've got to call next week regarding something, put the reminder in your phone. Obviously, you can and should also use your phone to text and email your clients, and vice-versa. If you have a customer who gives you "the creeps", you can text their phone number through several free web-based text messaging services so they never get your cell phone number. Google "free web-based texting".

- Make sure your phone is connected to all your social media accounts. Pinterest, LinkedIn, Facebook, Twitter, YouTube—whatever it is, put that app there, and stay active on those networks. Make it your sales lifeline—your relationship hub.

- You can also do text management during the sale. If you're on a demo drive while selling a car, for example, the customer might have a question like, "Can I get this in red?" or, "What's the best price?"

Simply say, "Mr. or Mrs. Customer, let me just text that condition back to management, and I'm sure they can get started on it before we get back." (Make sure you are not driving.)

- This will do a few things. They will stop asking you because you've sent it to your management. They will also be more inclined to come back into the building after the test drive since they believe management is already working on their request.

- Since management gets a heads-up on what's coming down the pike, they will have more time to work that deal for you.

- Video testimonials are another good use of your smartphone. People love to be famous. Record video testimonials any time you can, and absolutely post them on your YouTube channel or company page.

• You can also use your smartphone as a scanner or for QR codes.

• Sometimes, depending on where you are, it is much easier to take a picture of a document and email it to yourself to print out than it is to actually make it all the way back to a photocopier. There may even be apps available for this as well.

• Make sure that you keep your smartphone address books and contact lists up-to-date, and that you've got full information in there.

• Learn how to use address books properly. For example, if you wanted to send a mass text or email to all of your truck customers saying you need used trucks, or to promote a truck sale that is happening, you would want your contacts stored and sorted by category of what they bought, when they bought it, etc. It is important to understand how to use address books properly so that you have them organized in such a way that will make it easy for you to send blanket texts or emails when you need to. A very simple process I use is to put both their first and last names in the "first name" field. I then enter either the vehicle type and model they bought (New Ford F150 Truck), or I put if they are a "Prospect" in the "last name" field. Typing any of those keywords in the name field will pull up all the similar records. Just make sure you obtain consent to do this sort of marketing to your clients.

• You can even use your smartphone to take pictures of specials you are running, and then post those specials on your social media pages or blast out to your targeted contacts.

• Taking a short video of a live walk around the store or your product is another great idea. That way, anytime someone gives you an email address or a cell phone number, you can send them the YouTube video of you walking around the store by simply pasting the link. If you start sending these videos to all of your sales calls, email leads, people who walk out, and "be-back" attempts, you will discover that these videos are powerful. YouTube videos are a free way to dramatically improve your SEO.

• If you do personalized videos, an important point to remember is to not put the customer's last name in the video. For privacy reasons, personalize it with first name only.

• Because people have short attention spans, make it no longer than 59 seconds. And when you upload it to YouTube, make sure that you properly fill out the title and tags field so that this video can be easily found and leveraged.

• Set up the proper Google reference and tag names so that your video gets you into the SEO rankings (organic Internet searches based on keywords and terms). You want to make sure in the title and tags fields that you include the complete product name, make, model and year (if applicable), your first and last name, and the company's name.

• Remember to never delete those videos from YouTube. Even if you're only doing four or five videos a month, you will have about fifty to sixty YouTube videos up in a year. Don't underestimate the immense power in your market place this kind of video volume will give you over time.

- If you are a manager, you should try to ensure that every sales and service rep is using the same smartphone and carrier. Be it an iPhone, Blackberry, Android, Samsung or other, this could easily be chosen by a vote. Sharing a common carrier and type of smartphone will allow for more data-sharing and CRM applications to work more effectively on a group level for your sales team.

Duane Brain Tip

Reader, if the company helps pay for any portion of their sales teams' phones or phone bills, then it follows that the company has the right to back up those phones at a common database. That way, should a member of the sales team leave, the sales manager will still have all the salesperson's customer and prospect information backed up and available for the company.

- One last point I want to stress is that if you are using your personal smartphone as your primary CRM tool, back it up regularly. I recommend you back it up to your PC as well as to the "cloud" since those two systems back up your data in different ways. There is nothing more frustrating or frightening than losing your phone and knowing that you might have permanently lost some or all of your valuable data.

- Also, if anyone sends you screenshots of chats and conversations, know that you are only seeing a small portion of the conversation—if it is indeed the real conversation. Contacts can be saved under any name or telephone number, so take whatever anybody sends you with a grain of salt. Also, know that anyone who gossips about others will gossip about you, in time.

These are some great tips to make sure you're making the best use of your smartphone device as a CRM. A very small portion of salespeople use their CRM/smartphones properly, and when you start to become part of that small percentage, it will turn into a valuable habit that will give you another advantage over salespeople who don't.

Be enjoyable, valuable and memorable after delivery. Start to attract and pursue business. And please, after having read all this information, don't just wait for business to walk through the door.

"Time is the only equal opportunity employer there is...."

Duane Marino

CHAPTER 11

Power #4: Your Power of Effective Use of Time

Your next sales power is your power of effective use of time to build relationships. If you're going to provide better customer service, improve your use of sales language, and apply the tools of your trade to become memorable and valuable to your customer base, you will find that this all takes time.

Time is the only equal opportunity employer there is; it doesn't care who you are or what your background is. No matter how you measure or represent it—12 months, 52 weeks, 365 days, 24 hours, a day of 1440 minutes or 86,400 seconds—time is like a bank account. You have to decide how you will use your allotment—if you will just spend it, waste it or invest it—and you will never get any more time in a day than the person next to you does. However, you certainly can learn to use your time differently and more wisely.

Waste of time

We have all experienced wasting time, and if you're wasted moments have a habitual, repetitive pattern, then you may have some time traps you've fallen into. A time trap is any activity that takes you away from being as productive as possible, especially during your money hours. My "time trap audits" show that the average salesperson easily wastes or allows two hours of unproductive time to slip between his or her fingers on any given workday. Two hours could even be considered a conservative estimate, as in many cases it may easily be more than that. If you're wasting two hours a day for five days a week, and you do that for four weeks a month, you are wasting forty hours of precious, non-renewable, unproductive time every month. A keen self awareness of how you spend, waste or invest your time is crucial and rare. Think of what you could do with that time. In the light of that, you may want to do something to improve your effective use of time.

"The past is over, and the future is yet to come. The best thing about the present is that it's here now."

—*John Grinder*

What Determines Our Use of Time?

I believe there are really only three things that determine how we use our time. They are:

- Our values
- Our interests
- Our goals

One of our upcoming powers will be the Power of Focus. When you become a better goal setter, you automatically start managing your time better. After all, we always make time for things that are important to us, so being aware and focused on what's important to you is fundamental when you are trying to make progress in any area of your life.

Motivational Rituals

My father instilled in me that appearance mattered, and even as a machinist, he always took good care of his work boots.

When I go to work, the last thing I do before I leave my home or hotel is wipe down my shoes to get my head in the game and so that I look the part. That tells me that I'm leaving to go to work. The very first thing I do when I come home is kick them off, a conscious gesture that tells me I'm now at home.

You need an anchor or ritual like that which allows you to flip a switch inside you and tell you that you're changing modes or settings. One of the worst things you can do in this business is have too much personal and professional spillover.

Too many salespeople never succeed because they have not learned to effectively compartmentalize their life. Instead, they bring their home life to work, and their work life home, resulting in being ineffective in both areas. As a matter of fact, because they aren't fully present at home or work, they can't really enjoy much in either setting.

You need an anchor or ritual like that which allows you to flip a switch inside you and tell you that you're changing modes or settings.

Duane Brain Tip

Reader, there is a saying in the car business: "Go to work to work." I have never really liked this. Most people can't go to work to work because they have never learned how to leave their home at home!

Three Ways of Spending Your Time to Build Your Business

As mentioned in the previous chapter, there are only three ways you can spend your time to build your business. They are:

- You can wait for traffic

- You can pursue appointments

- You can attract repeats and referrals

- The average salesperson spends the majority of his or her time waiting around, and very little time trying to pursue or attract. An above-average salesperson spends the majority of his or her time trying to attract, and then pursue, thereby eliminating time wasted on waiting around for business to come in by itself. Plus, anyone who comes in asking for you is more likely to buy, usually pays you a little more and is a lot less stressful to deal with. Appointments, repeats, and referrals will set you free and ignite your income. Powerful use of time in this area makes you much more effective.

The best or perhaps only way to convert time into money is by reducing or eliminating your unproductive time. It means going to work to sell, and not just to wait for something to happen. How you spend your time is your ultimate personal choice. Again, it all depends on your own personal values, your own interests, and your own goals. The day you decide to keep your paper appointment calendar on your desk is the same day you say "I'm interested in more appointments!"

My mother is a master organizer and very proficient at everything she does. She taught me that what you do in between customers is at least as important—or maybe more so—than what you do when you're with them. It's like going to the gym or working out to improve your health. What you do outside of the gym—how you manage your lifestyle, your nutrition, hydration, sleep, and your stress—is just as important as what you do once you're in the gym, perhaps even more so.

Victim vs. Victor

That being said and done, let's take a look at the difference between a victim and a victor. A victim would be someone who doesn't take charge of his day, his time, or his environment. He would wait around for walk-in traffic and hope for the best, and blame everything and everyone for a bad month, but never blames themselves. On the other hand, a victor makes the day happen. He proactively takes charge of his day, his time, and his success. Take a look at the daily activity summaries on the next two pages of a victim versus a victor, and notice the difference in their attitudes and in the ways they spend their time. I have lived as both a victim and a victor, so I wrote them in the first person.

A Day in the Life of a Victim

8:00am: Wake up to my alarm, hit snooze several times, and drag myself out of bed. Start the day with instant coffee, no breakfast, no planning, no exercise. Run out the door at the last minute starting my day on a chase. No written goals or to-do list for the day, just did "what I had to do." Motivation for working was to "pay the bills."

8:30: Rush to work, pick up a muffin, donut or fast food breakfast along the way, and smoke a cigarette. Listen to the news about some tragedy, or call an energy drainer.

9:00: Get to work one minute before start time, park in whatever spot is still available. Chat with a negative coworker, criticize the boss, laugh about our jobs and customers, and spend thirty minutes figuring out who will go for coffee and donuts at the 10:00 break.

9:30: Mindlessly surf the Internet, gossip, and wait around for traffic, expecting business to just appear.

10:30: Spend thirty minutes figuring out what to eat and who will pick up lunch.

12:00pm: Lunch alone in lunch room or pick up some fast food and eat it in the car.

1:00: Read the newspaper about more bad news, talk about how bad it all is, wait around for traffic, and talk about nothing important or productive.

1:30: Spend thirty minutes figuring out who will go for coffee and donuts at 2pm.

2:30: Have a major energy crash that lasts at least an hour, take a donut and coffee break, and maybe have a cigarette to "recharge".

5:00: Do nothing during the last hour, just waiting it out until it's time to go home.

6:00: Leave no matter what and listen to more bad news on the radio, or phone an energy taker.

7:00: Eat whatever is in the fridge for dinner while watching TV, make a half-hearted attempt at personal/family time, and pass out on the couch with the TV still on.

11:45: Get off the couch and drag yourself to bed.

12:00am: Lie in bed sleepless and feeling discouraged, knowing the day was unproductive, and complaining about the day before finally falling asleep.

That past personal "era" is nicknamed in my home as "Woodfern Road," and it was neither fun nor productive.

A Day in the Life of a Victor

5:15am: Wake up rested and ready to go without the alarm. Morning Power Hour: read personal emails and e-newsletters; take vitamins and supplements, power shake and healthy breakfast. Review written goals, gratitudes and motivations. Ask oneself, "How do I want my day to be?"

6:15: Work out, shower, pack healthy snacks/lunch, filtered water, dress for success, get a day's supply of business cards and name tag.

7:15: Drive to work, ask oneself, "What do I HAVE to do today?" Pick up a customer's car for service, drink a cup of green tea, and listen to good humor, some great music, or simply enjoy the silence. Give oneself a positive pep talk and affirmations of one's skills or aspirations.

7:45: Get to work early, park at the back of the lot, walk the lot, help with service overFLOW, say "hi" to everyone in all departments, and breathe deeply.

9:00: Confirm today's appointments and deliveries, check emails, review plan for the day.

9:30: Watch for traffic, but if none, contact possible clients by whatever means and log all quality contact prospects; target to make at least five to ten new contacts daily. Ask oneself after every personal interaction, "How did I do?"

12:30pm: Eat a healthy lunch with technicians, a coworker or a networker. Find five appropriate used cars in the mall parking lot and put my business card with the note "I'm interested in your car" under their wiper blade. Have three brief, random conversations throughout the day, outside of work, each concluding with handing them one's business card while saying, "Great chatting, and you never know!" (Whoever said, "Don't talk to strangers," was obviously not a salesperson.)

1:15: If you're tired, take a fifteen-minute power nap. Then surf your virtual inventory and breathe deeply to energize.

1:45: Again watch for traffic, but if none, contact possible clients by whatever means, and log all quality contact prospects. Continue the target to make at least five to ten new contacts daily.

6:00: Confirm tomorrow's deliveries, review remaining week/month, check emails, pull up customer's service appointment list for tomorrow and offer a pick-up service.

6:30: Leave only once things are done and organized for the next day. Listen to non-theatrical news on the way home. Ask oneself, "How do I want my evening to be?"

7:00: Avoid TV, eat a healthy dinner, and enjoy personal or family time.

9:00: Go for a gratitude walk, review the day, plan for tomorrow, align goals.

9:30: Personal or family time.

10:00: In bed, feeling a good tiredness knowing the day was productive, and grateful for another day. Before sleeping, do twenty minutes of reading or watching videos on YouTube, with my smartphone, of motivational, spiritual or educational material. Ask oneself, "What are two things I did well and two things I could have done better?"

From the ages of fifteen to twenty-three, I was guilty of spending the majority of my time very much like a victim. Because I am speaking from my own experience, I can very much relate to that type of habitual behavior and attitude, and I know first hand the slow and almost undetectable drain it creates on you over a number of years. It's not very productive, and it's not very inspiring for you or anyone close to you.

Then, by making a conscious decision to change my habits and behavior, including how I chose to see things, who I spent my time with, and what I read, I moved over to the victor side. These days, I spend the vast majority of my day like a victor, and I love it.

Duane Brain Tip

Reader, I rarely watch TV. I believe TV is a massive time-waster, exposes us and our families to all kinds of fearful, negative information, normalizes crazy values and installs false beliefs. Study the current state of affairs and ownership of mass media, and you may make the same decision.

I strongly believe that eventually you are compensated for the degree of activity that you put into any given task. If you're very active and focused, if you make those contacts, build your skills and do your job, it's going to pay off. If you regularly analyze and cultivate your attitude, you will be rewarded for it.

Even if you go to work, and you're highly productive as far as your activity goes, but you don't sell anything that day, you're still going to go home feeling a "good" tired. You know that you tried, that you did the best that you could. Those fifty people you talked to today just might each talk to one person that night, which makes another fifty people, and one of them may contact you.

So by contacting fifty people, you're actually connecting indirectly with at least one hundred. And it is possible that out of the other group of fifty, somebody is actually in the market for your product. It may seem random and indirect, but the sales gods will always compensate you for any additional activity that you invest in your career. Add the effect that social media has on this, and by contacting 50 people a day, you may be indirectly tapping into the psyche of hundreds of people.

Remember that you need to change your habits to spend your time more effectively. Take a look at the Victim and Victor sheets to really get an idea of how you can use your time more productively in this business if you decide to. You will feel better for it, your morale will be higher, and you will have the income to enjoy the life you want to live.

As a bonus, by reading this book, you get a free pass to MarinoTV. Just log on to www.DuaneMarino.com, and go to MarinoTV. We have posted videos with almost 2000 tips like you've been reading here. I hope you take advantage of this. Check some of these things out for yourself, and create a great day for yourself and anyone you care about!

CHAPTER 12

Power #5: Your Power of Understanding Body Language

Your next sales power is the power of understanding body language to build relationships. I have found that understanding the nuances of body language was one of the differences that made a big difference in my professional and personal effectiveness. When you deeply understand body language, you read people better, and you can project better messages to them. The words we use comprise only a small portion of our communications. The majority of our message comes through in our tone, our inflection, and our body language. The better you are at projecting and reading body language, the better you will be as a communicator, a salesperson, a parent and a friend. It is truly a universal skill.

A quick search on Google and YouTube will reveal some really incredible and interesting information on body language, which can be very useful in sales.

Understanding Body Language

A good salesperson can use his or her understanding of body language to assess whether the person he is speaking to likes and respects him or not. You really can't sell anything to anyone unless you first get them to like or respect you, as they won't listen to you otherwise. As a first step, there are some things you can do during the sale to check if someone is actually listening to you or not, which is crucial because listening is the by-product of someone liking or respecting you. This may sound strange, but one way to see if someone likes you (even a little) is to "accidentally" drop your pen or some other small item. Someone who likes you will try to help you out by at least pointing this out or will bend over to make an attempt to pick it up for you. But if they just look at you, look down, and look back at you with no attempt whatsoever to help you get your pen back, it's not only rude but also a good sign that they don't particularly like or respect you. This is not always the case, but it serves well as a general rule of thumb and is just one of many examples of how you can use body language in a tactical way.

A good tip to see who is paying attention (and thus, who likes or respects you) is to act as if you lost track of the subject matter, and ask the person during the sale to remind you what you were just talking about. You could say something like, "I'm sorry, where were we?" or, "I was just distracted, what exactly was I saying again?"

It's like a pop quiz on what was being talked about, that you can use to assess if the other person has been listening. Remember, if someone has been listening, it means that they probably like and respect you.

Another way of using body language to assess a person's like or dislike of you is by mirroring them to see if they, in turn, will also mirror you. A person who likes you will tend to mimic what you do, in an unconscious demonstration of emphasizing the kinship they feel towards you.

As mentioned earlier, this is called *entraining*. For example, if you scratch your nose, it would not be uncommon for someone who respects and likes you to scratch their face as well within a few seconds.

Another communication cue you should be alert to is whether they are sharing any private or personal information with you. If a person likes you, they will be more open to sharing the kinds of personal details of their lives with you that they would normally reserve only for people they trust. If they are, it's a great sign that they feel good about you.

If they like or respect you, they'll be able to listen to you. If you can get them to respond in a positive manner in the ways described above, then your probability of closing is in your favor. Great salespeople are great readers and projectors of body language. Other simple ways to ensure people are listening to you:

- Ask them questions
- Use their name occasionally
- Keep the conversation relevant
- Keep notes while they talk
- Vary the pace and volume of your speech
- Use visuals to make your point

Three Body Language Signals to Look for

There are three major body language signals that you should watch for as intently as a lion watches the gazelle he is hunting. They are as follows:

The Look of Sudden Positive Realization

This is a major buying signal to look out for. You're talking to a customer about a sale, when suddenly they open their eyes wider, subtly smile and then shift their center of gravity forward or backward little bit. Or they gasp, smile, lean their head back and say something like, "Wow, good point. I didn't think about that."

Even if not accompanied by verbal expression, if you see a body language gesture like that, you are seeing the look of Sudden Positive Realization. Try to close the sale now. You do this by asking a trapping "double bind either/or" closing question.

"So, Mr. Buyer, if we handled that, would you want to pick it up this afternoon or tonight? Do you want to put it in your name or your wife's?"

Do this while you smile and nod subtly. If that trap is well timed, and if you read that body language correctly, you're probably going to close the sale right then and there. It doesn't so much matter where you are in your sales process; what's important is that their body language has signaled that they might be at their peak of interest and that all the conditions are present for them to say "yes" to you right then and there.

Put your head down, write down or type their conditions on your screen and whatever it is they just picked in your alternate choice questions, draw a check mark, and ask for their OK. Then ask them if they would like to secure their offer with a credit card, debit card or cash, put your hand out, and be quiet.

Always close in a gentle and polite way, and always leave yourself a way out, just in case it doesn't work.

The Look of Sudden Negative Realization

This is the second look you need to be aware of, and it is the exact opposite of the first. You'll see a sudden "jolt" as your customer breaks eye contact and looks away, often down. He may shake his head from side to side, in the opposite of a nodding motion, or shift his center of gravity to one side. He suddenly looks upset or even sad, and it may just be a very small and fast micro expression. This is a clear signal that you've done something wrong.

If you see this, you want to quickly start asking questions like, "I'm sorry, what I meant was…" "Can we go back over that?" "Let me just rephrase this," or "what are you thinking?"

The look of Sudden Negative Realization is your cue that there has been a blunder and that you need to find out what it was and fix it before you can move forward. Both of the above looks should be used as major barometers to help guide you through the sales process.

The "Happy Trance"

This is the third look you need to keep an eye out for. I call it the "Happy Trance" because that's what it looks like when it lights up someone's face. It's that smiling, dreamy expression people will get from time to time when they think of something very pleasurable to them. If it occurs while you happen to be describing a particular feature, advantage or benefit of the product, it means you've got them where they live. Whatever it is that you are saying right now is really resonating with them. This "look" tells you that they are actually seeing themselves using the item and that you've really connected with them on this point and at their level. When you see that very happy trance, you are watching them clearly enjoy a moment of reverie regarding the future use of your product. Close the sale now as it is obvious most of the buying puzzle has been put together for your buyer.

This is a great time for you to ask another trapping "either/ or double bind" question. "So, Mr./Mrs. Buyer, if we handled your question about the installation, would you want the blue one or the red one? Do you want to take it on the sixty-month term, or do you want to go for seventy-two?"

You always want to close by asking an either/or two choice question, and if you've read things right, they will pick one, and you'll close the sale. Obviously only pick two things that are feasible from your perspective. The two choices creates the illusion of choice for your buyer, and whatever one they pick results in us closing the sale and them getting on with their lives and enjoying our product!

In addition to paying attention to these signals, it is also important to watch for other things that can provide important clues about your prospect's degree of engagement in the sales and buying process.

A tool called *calibration* will assist you with this. Calibration is the skill of assessing how a person normally communicates, so that you can use that as a baseline to compare it to any changes you observe. It's funny to watch someone trying to hold back on all body language cues, because, to a skilled eye, that "stillness" is communicating plenty in and of itself.

There is another tool called *sensory acuity* that you can use to assess your sales cycle and gather clues about your prospect. Sensory acuity is the art of using all of your senses to be alert to the little things that most people miss in terms of body language signals and cues. When talking to your customer, the two key things to look for in this regard are matches or mismatches; or *congruities and incongruities*. For example, if a person's facial expression is incongruous to his verbal language, or if his or her body language doesn't match up to the words they are saying, or if you aren't actually sure what somebody is saying, go with the body language before you let their words mislead you.

Sooner or later, what a person really thinks or feels will reveal itself with some aspect of their body language, even if they are verbalizing something completely different.

The following are the primary body language signals to watch for, some of which I mentioned earlier:

The first vital clue is found in facial expressions; in particular, *microexpressions*. A microexpression is a tiny, lingering expression or a very quick flash of expression that someone gets on his or her face. It usually lasts for a quarter of a second to half a second before it disappears again.

The microexpression is a "tell" that shows what a person is truly feeling. It is that emotional expression on a person's face that occurs in a quick flash before their conscious mind has a chance to catch up to what they are revealing to you. Remember emotion travels much faster than thought through our nervous system. It briefly shows their true emotion just before moving into another facial expression that may or may not be congruent to the previous one.

If you pay close attention, you will see not only the obvious facial expressions, but also these tiny, fast microexpressions. These small flashes are the ones to watch out for since the major muscle ones can be faked.

For example, a person can use a practiced smile to look happy when he or she really is not. And that practiced smile will not involve the overall deep facial muscle coordination and eye sparkle of a sincere smile. Their microexpression, however, will tell you a very different story. Just like in a game of poker, that flash of a microexpression provides the "tell" of how someone is really feeling. It happens the moment something they think of, hear, or see "registers" with them on a preconscious level.

The microexpression never lies. Look for it very closely. It will tell you how someone really feels about you and the product during the course of the sale.

Pay attention to the tone of a person's voice, and, in particular, to any *changes in voice tone*.

The next important body language cue is *eye movements*. When people are confused, they tend to look around in figure eight or circular patterns. This is how they look when they just can't put something together—when one's mind just can't find or coordinate the information it needs.

On the other hand, when a person feels certain about the information they have, you will find that they maintain a relatively steady gaze, and they will be rather quick to answer your question. Their eyes won't move, and there isn't much time spent answering as they don't need to process or internally locate the information.

If they suddenly start blinking or averting their eyes, they are probably not comfortable with the conversation.

When people's pupils dilate in a conversation, it means that they are very interested in what they are seeing or what you are saying.

When their pupils become smaller, this means they are

not very interested in what is happening. Being able to recognize the meanings of different eye movements will make you a more effective communicator. And, unless they have been extensively trained or are pathological liars, eye movements during fluid conversations are nearly impossible to fake.

These days, TV high stakes poker players are allowed to wear hats and sunglasses because the players of today learned their trade on computers and have never had to learn the science and art of body language. This is one of the reasons a professional salesperson should never wear sunglasses without permission during the sale as it projects that you are trying to hide something. Also, chewing gum or smoking during the sale is a no-no unless you are joining in with your happy prospect who offered it to you, and you are not visible to the rest of the showroom.

Center of gravity changes, which are shifts in how a person holds their body, can also provide important clues. When someone is fairly certain of what they are saying, they will lean in, even if it is very slightly. If they are not sure of something, they will lean back. If they are confused or concerned, they will move from side to side.

Time lag tells you something about how much thought a person is giving to your question. The longer it takes someone to answer a question, the more thought they are putting into it, or they want you to believe they are putting into it. None of this has to be about finding out if somebody is telling you the truth or lying; it is just the reality of how our thought processes work. Understanding this will make you a much more empathetic and effective communicator.

Proximity is a measure of how close a person stays to things, and is another body signal to note. If the buyer really likes someone or something, he likes to be close to it.

If I am planning on buying a car, I'll stay closer to the car I'm thinking of buying. I'll stay closer to the worksheet if I like the numbers. As soon as I stop liking things, I'll start moving or turning away from them. You'll notice things like that in terms of people's changes in proximity.

Directional body orientation or pointing is another body signal. No matter what he may be saying, if your prospect starts to orient his body toward your door with his feet, hips, shoulders, or face, he is looking to go home. People normally rotate their body in the direction they intend on taking next, or where they are subconsciously focused.

If you see even so much as a micro-glance at a watch, you have to recognize that they are probably getting ready to leave, and you will have to change the things you're doing in order to regain their attention.

If a person really likes you, they will begin to demonstrate what I call **natural global entrainment** with you. They will begin to mirror your voice tone, your movements, your sense of humor, your interests, values, and goals. If they are simply trying to influence you, the entrainment won't feel natural.

Blushing and flushing can also occur as a physical response to what is happening in the environment.

Blushing is actually a result of an increase in blood pressure. Your diaphragm tightens up, and if your skin capillaries are closer to the surface, you will tend to blush more easily. Also, the lighter the skin, the more visible the blush.

A person will blush because he or she is literally tightening up inside. It's harder to breathe when the diaphragm tightens up. If you are a blusher, practice relaxing and breathing through your belly to eliminate that "tell".

Flushing, on the other hand, is when a person suddenly loses all the color in their face. Blood isn't getting to their head.

If you see even so much as a micro-glance at a watch, you have to recognize that they are probably getting ready to leave, and you will have to change the things you're doing in order to regain their attention.

While blushing is usually related to nervousness, anger or embarrassment, flushing is a sign of extreme anxiety or fear. When someone is flushing, and starting to feel ill, having them lie down will allow blood back into their head.

A **change in breathing** is another body language sign. People who are very relaxed breathe a certain way. If they become nervous or agitated, then they start to breathe a different way. In fact, it is the pace, depth and location of our breathing that leads us into different states, as anyone who has studied martial arts, yoga or meditation can attest. A very deep and rapid way of entraining with someone to create almost instant rapport is to match their breathing.

The last point is **talking hands**. Many people use specific and situational, individual and cultural hand gestures. When you communicate similarly with your hands to these people and are more matched and expressive with your body language, you will be more effective as a salesperson and understood better by them.

Myself and most highly successful people are tremendously effective communicators; not only with our language, but with our body language as well. And that's why this is one of our sales powers.

Study these tips, and then go out and experience them in any social situation you find yourself in. I can tell you first hand that as you start to master them simultaneously, your sales will go up, your average transaction time will go down, your profits will increase, your stress levels will fall, and the quality of all your relationships will become much richer.

That's the power of body language, and it is a major power.

CHAPTER 13

Power #6: Your Power of Focus

Now let's take a look at our last and perhaps greatest power, the power of focus to build great relationships. Making a daily commitment to create and maintain relationships with your customers starts with you making the decision to do so.

"Everything is a state of mind."

—*Tony Robbins*

Best Time to Sell

When is the best time to sell something? We as salespeople know that the best time to sell is right after you've just sold something. Why? Because that's when you are still holding in your entire neurology the vision, beliefs, state and strategy of a sale! You've got a very recent blueprint of a sale in your mind and a great biochemical FLOW of endorphins in your body. You've got a lot of sales energy and confidence, and people pick up on that vibration. Imagine if you could feel like that every day, instantly and at will, even when you're not selling. Learning how to activate and motivate yourself as well as maintain this high level of sales energy is the purpose of this chapter.

The first thing you need to learn to do is how to avoid the trap of falling into the negative energy that can get generated when you aren't selling. When you lack "sales energy", it actually depletes the customer's buying energy, and, chances are, they won't feel like buying anything from you. The rule that applies here is that you can't give anything in life if you don't first have it yourself. If you ask me for a wrench, I can't give you a wrench unless I have a wrench to give. If I ask you for some buying energy, you can't give me buying energy unless you have sales energy.

Winning More and Losing Less

Fundamentally, humans are driven by some very simple motivations. There are really only two reasons that we will do something: to avoid pain or to gain pleasure. Some of us love to win more than we hate to lose; some of us hate to lose more than we love to win. In sales, it's important that you know which one of those you are as it will affect a lot about the way you sell and how you should set goals. This is a derivative of your need to avoid pain and gain pleasure, and it's one of the most basic things that defines how you play your sales game and how you play life.

Humans want to be healthy, wealthy and happy, and we all want to avoid suffering. So we know that we should think, plan and work towards the realization of a better future. If we don't set a game plan and an end goal for ourselves, or if we fail to plan for the future, we may lack a sense of purpose.

What is interesting is that, for better or worse, you use your past to influence your future. Being aware of this can help you select the parts of your past experiences that will help you create a better future outcome.

Take a moment to think about the things you've lost or gained along the way and of some of the pains and pleasures that you've had. Your game plan for the future should be along the lines of focusing on what you can control and working out how you can avoid some of those past pains to gain greater future pleasure. How can you win more and lose less?

By trying to use your own past setbacks as "teachable moments", you can get some positive meaning from almost any problems you've had. In this way, you can get some leverage to motivate yourself and move in a better direction "customized" and individualized to you. And there are really never any mistakes if you've learned something.

What Successful People Do

Successful people have trained themselves to replay their victories, learn from their losses, and move on!

Unsuccessful people do the opposite: they replay their losses; they don't learn much from their victories, and they never move on, living in their negative past moments and lost sales. Successful people also avoid negativity like the plague, because that's basically what it is!

Try to learn something from every sale lost and made. And remember, rejection is a feeling; people saying, "No," is a reality. Keep in mind the tenacity formula (SW, SW, SW, N!) "Some **Will**", "Some **Won't**", "**So What**", and "**Next!**"

Life Seasons

In addition to compartmentalizing your life and leaving

your home at home and your work at work, realize that your life has seasons. Some years, you've got to work harder than others, and some days of the week, you've got to work longer than others. Sometimes professional and personal seasons don't match up, and some periods in your life and business will be more challenging.

I experienced years of very intense mental and emotional activity after my daughter was born. Not only was I working and traveling a lot, but I was mastering new skills, creating new materials, improving my body and mind, overcoming some huge personal and financial obstacles, starting my businesses, and developing a software product.

I have a lengthy personal story as to how I ended up in the training business, and most of my reasons were based around trying to get out of pain. I can tell you it certainly was not easy being on the road alone and trying to find the resources I needed to fix myself, create a business and be really successful at what I wanted to do. But I had many reasons to keep plugging away and working hard on both my business and myself.

What I committed to then was that when I was at home, I would make sure I was *really* home. If I was only home for two or three days a week, I made sure that my children and family were my first priority and that they got all my time. However, during my most intense times of development, there are pictures of me with my kids on my lap blowing out candles while my laptop was open on the table during birthday dinners! There were only so many hours in a day, and I had to do what I had to do!

Back then, I didn't do much of anything outside of the house, and I didn't take any time to pursue any of my other passions like working out, yoga, taking classes, golf, soccer, or spending time with my very small circle of close friends.

I made whatever sacrifices I had to so that I could create my business and build my family. That was it because that was the season I was in. I simply could not risk diluting myself into what I thought were non-essential, unproductive activities.

It is pretty illogical for a farmer to try to pick fruit in the spring. In the spring, you've got to turn the dirt and plant the seeds. You've got to take care of the garden in the summertime. But in the fall, you reap the benefits from all the work you did during the previous seasons—and of course, there is always winter where you take stock and rest.

But it is important to recognize that in life, sales, and business, there are seasons. What season are you in now? Sometimes, life throws you into different seasons unexpectedly, and the daily weather is always uncertain. Try to learn the skills to keep your internal weather as calm and clear as possible so you can navigate your life with greater ease.

I feel blessed to have come across the people, teachings and philosophies that help me do just that. When the student is ready, the teachers appear!

Life will always throw you some twists and turns, and there isn't much you can do about that. But if you don't have any idea as to where you're going, it's just never going to work out for you. You'll always be lost. You can't always choose which cards life will deal you, but you can try to control the decisions you make and the meaning of the game! Take some time to step back and take a look at where you are going.

Life's Compass

Knowing what general direction you are headed is very useful. Is it the right direction for you? What is important to you? Where do you want to go next? Just like a sailor navigating the seven seas, you need a compass to help point you in the direction you want to go.

Life will always throw you some twists and turns, and there isn't much you can do about that. But if you don't have any idea as to where you're going, it's just never going to work out for you. You'll always be lost. You can't always choose which cards life will deal you, but you can try to control the decisions you make and the meaning of the game! Take some time to step back and take a look at where you are going. Are you still headed in the right direction? Sometimes, you need to take another look at the goals you have drawn up for yourself, and possibly reassess them and your rate of progress towards them. Are you getting closer to accomplishing those things you wanted to achieve? Are they appropriate goals?

As I write this chapter, my children are recovering from some brutal sports injuries. They are both on full soccer scholarships; my daughter is in Louisiana and my son in Iowa. My daughter is recovering from a complete rupture to her Achilles tendon and my son from a major concussion. Just as they got near the top of their ladders, which took years to climb, life and circumstances have thrown them a major curve ball. I am enormously proud of them both, and it is amazing to watch them use the same skills they developed to achieve phenomenal academic and athletic successes towards recreating their own futures in light of these terrible injuries and setbacks.

Life's Map

A compass won't do you much good without a map. Whereas a compass will point you in the correct general direction, a map lays out the details of your journey—the actual activities you need to do to move in the direction of your goal. You need those important details, not just the overall picture, to get where you want to be.

You need to be able to focus on where you are headed, or you will get distracted and get off course. Take driving your car as an example. When you're driving somewhere, you have your sights set ahead of you. You most likely keep your front window clear and unobstructed so you can see where you are going. While you focus on that front window, you don't tend to spend much time looking at your rear view mirror, especially if you're driving your car through heavy traffic at 100 mph.

Now imagine if your rear-view mirror were as big as your front window, and your front window were no bigger than the size your rear-view mirror is now, it wouldn't take you long to get disoriented. And sooner than later, you would be lost, confused, and stressed as you try to drive forward while looking back.

The point is, where you've been is actually irrelevant to where you're going. You want to focus on where you're headed and not get distracted by what's in your "rear-view mirror". Your future is not dictated by your past unless you choose to live there. However, the major things in your past that will help you today are your gratitudes and your learnings.

FLIP Method

I would like to introduce you to my FLIP method to help you succeed. "FLIP" is an acronym that you can always rely on to help you stay focused on achieving your goals and staying in the right state of mind.

"F" for Focus

In order to stay motivated and on your game, you want to focus on your desired outcome. You want to focus on things you want and avoid things that may distract you. Your energy FLOWs where your focus goes.

Focusing on what you want to avoid may sound odd, but as an example, I have a definite vision of how I *don't* want to retire. I do whatever I can today to make sure I don't retire that way. But I'm not feeding that negative vision by giving it any energy or fear. It's just a motivator that I use to remind myself of where I really don't want to end up after putting in decades of hard work. I am always moving away from that unpleasant picture in my attempt to avoid future pain.

I was blessed to have two uncles who demonstrated exactly how not to live, what not to drink and eat, how not to treat women, how not to spend money, and how not to behave towards a career.

While they prayed daily for someone to come down from the clouds to save them, I was realizing the tangible value of working on ourselves!

Since a small boy, these two "anti-heroes" showed me what

can happen to otherwise-intelligent and kind people who make some unforgiving errors of judgment. It wasn't until I was in my 30s that I realized how formative my exposure to them was for me.

While you are aware of what you don't want or won't tolerate, focus on what you do want and move towards it with energy and intention. While I always keep the "big picture" in mind, I also have a clear idea of how I would like my month, week and day to be. There are many things that I want to do for my family, my business, my support team, my customers, others and myself. If you focus, you really do increase the odds of getting what you want. As I have stated, I find it very valuable to focus on what you want (pleasure), and also focus on what you want to avoid (pain).

"L" for Language

In sports, internal language is referred to as "self-talk". It's what you say to yourself. External language, on the other hand, is what you say to others.

By changing your self-talk—what you say to yourself and how you say it—you can change your focus and your energy. Your repetitive, internal language will affect your external language, or how you speak to and interact with other people. This is very important in sales. You want to speak in an appropriate way to your potential buyer in the given situation. I use language in my seminars in lots of fun and creative ways to educate, motivate and provoke people in the room. As I am keenly in touch with people's body language, I will often talk in ways exactly opposite to what certain individuals want or expect to hear. I do this to challenge their own internal processes and the way they deal with adversity, being offended (which is really a decision and not an actual event) and situations they find unpleasant. Great salespeople are pliable, adaptable, non-judgmental, and have thick skin.

Just be aware of the close connection between internal self-talk and your communication with others. And this is another reason why understanding your body language and that of others is so powerful.

"I" for Intensity

Intensity is what we define as the stamina of the body and the mind. If you want to really blow your mind, read dozens of studies in the over 100-year-old science of quantum physics, which are showing that the mind may not be located in the brain!

The reality is that some people just can't put in a full day. They simply don't have the energy for it. They're not taking good enough care of themselves or may be ill. But intensity, stamina of body and mind are all important factors that you should cultivate and work on. It takes a lot of energy to sell well, and the last thing you want is to tire out in front of your buyer or before you can make it a great month.

"P" for Physiology

Physiology refers to the way you treat and relate to your body. There are certain things that people can do with their bodies to increase their energy level.

You'll notice that positive people tend to have good posture when they walk, and their faces are fairly clear or focused. These are people whom you should emulate and model your physiological traits by.

There are several things you should avoid doing. Try not to look down, slouch, or have an unfriendly expression on your face. Don't defocus your eyes, frown or make a habit out of walking slowly; these things all send a signal to your brain to breath poorly and to steadily release a slew of feel-bad and unhealthy hormones such as cortisol.

Successful people walk with a pace, purpose, and good posture because it gives them, and others around them who are mirroring them, more energy. They keep their faces clear or even smiling, looking straight out or up. They are aware of and engaged in their immediate environment. If you can start to adopt this type of physiological behavior, you will find that you actually feel more alive and alert.

As mentioned earlier, martial arts, yoga, and meditation teach us energizing body positions and breathing. If you've ever had any experience with the Eastern philosophies, you will notice that this is what they focus on, and it is very useful in sales.

The other side of physiology addresses literally what we're made of, which is mostly water and oxygen. You can strengthen your own physiology by taking some deep breaths throughout the day and drinking plenty of clean water.

In the high-pressure business of sales, especially if it involves frequent travel or long hours, we can easily develop some unhealthy lifestyle habits. You can start to turn this around by simply drinking plenty of water and taking some deep breaths throughout the day to make sure you stay hydrated and oxygenated. This, in turn, will help retain your mental and physical stamina, you will be mentally sharp, and you will be able to maintain higher energy levels for longer periods of time. This will result in higher productivity levels, sales, and income.

Nutrition is another important factor. Pay attention to what you're putting in your mouth. Instead of thinking, "I've got to eat," or "I'm hungry," think in terms of nutrition. "What nutritious snack can I grab? How can I keep myself energized?" Simply make the best choice you can at the moment wherever you may be eating, and give some serious consideration to packing healthy snacks when you leave for work.

"To develop a strong body, keep it moving. To develop a strong mind, learn to keep it still."
—*Duane Marino*

Goals and gratitudes are important too. I started writing down my own goals and gratitudes on September 13th, 2001, two days after the 9/11 tragedy, following a Detroit Lions' football game that I attended with Bob Mohr, his brother, and John Kostakos. It was a very stressful time as I'm sure you can recall.

During the course of conversations we had that night (and everyone but me showing and sharing their written goals that they kept in their wallets), I was given the suggestion to write down my goals and gratitudes after I left the game. And this is exactly what I did in the hotel room I was sharing with John.

At the time, I was trying to get my personal and professional debts under control, and I didn't want to spend $100 on a hotel room of my own. And so, before falling asleep in that hotel room, I took out my notepad, and by the light of a small lamp, I wrote down my very first list of goals and gratitudes. I remember that moment like it was yesterday.

"If you can't enjoy what you have now, you won't enjoy more of it later."

—*Richard Bandler*

Since then, every few months, I take the time to rewrite my goals and gratitudes on a little card that I keep in my pocket. I then take a picture of it and set it as my screen background on my phone. Every day, I glance at it for about thirty seconds, and while I do that, I find that I feel energized and refocused. Then, for about 5 minutes, I review a matrix of principles and practices that I live by.

Remember that successful people only repeat what works. When you notice what is bringing good results, don't stop doing it, and don't change what you're doing. I've shared this concept of reviewing written goals, gratitudes, principles and practices with thousands of people, and I've gotten hundreds of emails and text messages back, telling me how effective it has been for them and others as well.

When it comes to putting your goals and gratitudes into writing, you should do it in your own handwriting. Don't type them out or put them on a computer. When you write them down in your own handwriting, you have a personal connection with that list every time you review it. Both of my children use this technique to help them stay focused on their lives and their goals. They will both tell you that their accomplishments are a direct result of having written down their goals and gratitudes, and by looking at them every morning on their wall cork board.

We have all been given to believe that there is a lot of "luck" involved in success, but let's not forget that "luck" mostly stands for **L**abor **U**nder **C**orrect **K**nowledge. If you think it's all astrology, you can't control where or when you were born, so work on you! Successful people do whatever it takes and keep working at it. By doing this, they create their own luck.

Success requires hard work, and the sad fact is that most people won't succeed simply because they give up. If you refuse to quit, you'll eventually be the last one standing, and the goal will be yours.

Beliefs

Remember that beliefs are like labels, and labels are an easy way for us to deal with the world. The labels we assign to things will drive our beliefs, and our beliefs and values control the amount of energy we will allow ourselves to invest in any person, goal, or activity that we label. Making sure that we assign the correct labels to things is very important to setting new goals for ourselves. If we assign the wrong importance to the wrong activity, we can lead ourselves away from, instead of closer to, our stated goals. Understanding more about what controls your beliefs is a great way to ensure you stay on the right track with your goal-setting activities.

There are three things that control our beliefs:

Our imagination—give yourself permission to imagine bigger and better things for yourself and our world.

Our experiences—we can choose to focus on what we want to learn from our experiences.

Information—especially in this digital age, there is a lot of informational material available out there, but much of it is untrue, downright misleading, or fear mongering, intentionally designed to keep you small. Make sure that whatever information you select for yourself is current, supportive, relevant, and accurate in today's world.

Our beliefs are also formed through hetero-suggestion and auto-suggestion. Hetero-suggestion has to do with how we pick up on other people's beliefs or opinions about us, whether directly or indirectly. For example, if there is someone in your life whose opinion means a lot to you, and they form a negative belief or opinion of you, this can actually cause you to feel insecure, and you may start to question yourself. Regardless of whether the beliefs and opinions of others are good or bad, valid or invalid, we tend to own and adopt them on a subconscious level.

Auto-suggestion, on the other hand, is the programming we give ourselves to what we believe we are capable of. The best antidote to negative hetero-suggestion is positive auto-suggestion. Auto-suggestion gives you the power to create a new world for yourself from the inside out. And, after all, improving yourself is an inside job.

When my daughter was nine years old, she decided she wanted to get a soccer scholarship. At the time, she was by far the worst player on her house league soccer team, and I almost told her not to bother. I'm so glad I understood enough about psychology at that point to not do that to her. Instead, I just gave her the flexibility and the ability to pick her own targets and goals in life, and I made the decision to support her in any way that I could.

As a child, my son was constantly tormented by cruel and ineffective coaching. But his self-talk was so powerful and congruent, he did whatever he had to do to prove his loser coaches wrong. And, as I mentioned earlier, both of them ended up going to college on full soccer scholarships through their own hard work and focus.

And for those of you who know a young athlete who wants a sports scholarship, the way to increase their odds is embedded in the language. It's a "scholarship", not a "sport-ship". So, the number-one thing to work on is academics. Having appropriate goals is everything!

It is important to remember that we are all a work in progress and that nothing is set in stone. But by fostering a great relationship with ourselves, reviewing our goals and gratitudes daily, understanding what we focus on, how we talk to ourselves, our internal and external language, our intensity, and our physiology, we can maintain a very high level of life and sales energy most days. And with a consistent focus, effort, and state of mind, you can achieve virtually anything!

Duane Brain Tip

Reader, a quick cautionary note about beliefs: most beliefs are driven by fear (a need for certainty in uncertain situations) and ego (a need to be right at all costs). If you are not careful, the same beliefs that made you, can trap you.

For example, anytime to you create a belief about anything, you must create a rule set and evidence to support that belief. In order to improve, you have to believe you can. But don't limit yourself to thinking you need certain things in place (superstition), certain people around you (dependency), or that you really know your ultimate goal (believing you should and can sell 30 cars a month will prevent you from selling 20, but also 40.) Beliefs can be a double-edged sword.

As I mentioned earlier, please go back to page 101, and rerate your mastery of your Six Sales Powers now, and see how your perceptions of your career and yourself have changed.

CHAPTER 14

Introspection

I want to conclude this book with some important thoughts. First off, I strongly recommend that you find a good peer group. When I was younger, once I started to figure out how I wanted to live and what work I wanted to excel at, I didn't really have a peer group to teach me and help me align what I wanted. I didn't even recognize the value of having one. I love my family, but my family was not able to help me with where I wanted to go. I also recognized that for things to change for me, lots of things had to change about me. I didn't have any business or sales gurus in my family. As a matter of fact, it's safe to say that I had the opposite when it came to business or sales success.

In my family, I had a lot of examples of how I didn't want to live; how I didn't want to retire; how I didn't want to treat other members of my family, and how I didn't want to treat my body. I would say I hit a whole new level of maturity when I realized that if I wanted a different life for myself I would need to find some different strategies and mentors. Without being judgmental towards others, I started on a very strong path of personal development. And also realized I needed some effective guidance in this matter.

The first peer group that I adopted was in the form of a virtual peer group of books, CDs, and workshops. Then I started to really watch what other people around me were doing and decided to model the best traits of my coworkers, bosses, clients and competition. I sought out people who were living at what I felt was my next level and created my own personal growth formula: R&Dx2 (Research and Development so I could Repeat and Duplicate what I needed at that time). I looked for business, sales, emotional, physical, psychological, financial, and family role models. And, as I've said three times now, when the student is ready, the teachers shall appear. They did for me, and they still do to this day.

Therefore, I ask you, "Does the peer group you have right now fully support your goals?" The only people you should share your goals with are those who will support you 100%, or those whom you're very sure you want to spite. These would be so-called friends, family members, coworkers and others who purposely hurt you, hold you down, keep you back or mislead you. I have always found this form of motivation especially invigorating.

If you want to spite someone, prove them wrong, and show them how worthwhile you are as a human being, hold that person in your mind while you burn the midnight oil. Make the extra calls, build your skills, work the extra hours, and be smart with your time and money. One day, you will imagine them saying to themselves, "Holy cow, look what you have become. Maybe I should've been kinder or gentler or more helpful or not so petty or jealous or selfish way back when because you have really become something!"

One day, you will take a deep, fulfilling breath, and say to yourself, "Hey look, I did it even though you said I couldn't or shouldn't or wouldn't be able to!" For me, there is perhaps no greater feeling than proving someone wrong. I have used this same thing to motivate those around me that I love. It's basic reverse psychology.

Again, you should only share your goals with people who will inspire you or motivate you to achieve them, whether it's through their support or through them telling you that you aren't capable. So double-check your peer group, create a real or imaginary mastermind group of people you look up to, and make sure it truly supports your goals and ambitions. If you don't already have a peer group, now is the time to start developing one.

"If the mind can conceive it and believe it, it can achieve it!"

—*Napolean Hill*

What Affects Our Success in Life?

There are three things that are going to determine your success levels:

You have to have a strong desire to learn.

You have to have a willingness to change.

You have to have the focus to execute, daily!

Any one of those three is not enough on its own. In fact, two out of three probably won't get you anywhere either.

Please take a moment and rate yourself out of ten in each of those three areas.

If you have a strong desire to learn and a very high focus to execute but no willingness to change, you're just going to end up frustrating yourself because you just keep using the same, and probably wrong, tools more aggressively.

If you have a low desire to learn, but a very strong willingness to change and a very strong focus to execute, you won't understand why things aren't working out for you. Because, although you want to change, you're blocking yourself from learning or experiencing anything new.

Lastly, if you have a strong desire to learn and a high willingness to change, but a low focus to execute consistently, then you're a great student, but you lack the focus and stamina to use your skills to get you where you want to be.

Top salespeople or business people have a tremendous desire to learn, an exceptional willingness to change, and a deep focus to execute.

My Story—Evolve or Dissolve

In life, you have to remember that if you don't evolve, you will eventually dissolve.

In the 8th grade, I was Class Valedictorian and the lead in the play. But when I started 9th grade, I was overwhelmed by the size of my high school and was just another anonymous freshman. Practically overnight, I went from what I felt was a hero down to a zero. This was very hard on me, and I had a hard time recovering from it. Already an introvert, I became very introverted for a long period after that.

To make matters even worse, I then got mixed up with what my family thought was the wrong crowd, and became an extreme introvert with a bad attitude. I did manage to always keep busy, had several concurrent jobs, worked hard at school, maintained a high GPA, and I stayed very active athletically.

But, because my family really didn't approve of my friends

and how they looked, I retaliated by cutting off nearly all communication with them out of stubbornness from the ages of about fifteen to twenty-three.

This became much worse when my family dynamic shifted as my closest sister, at that time, started dating a very negative, jealous and small-minded person who didn't like me. Remember earlier when I said I don't like being told what not to do? Well, that trait, which inspires me professionally, also destroyed my family relationships for some time. I lacked the maturity to know the difference between the productive and negative use of my own emotions.

During that time, I was just an angry kid. I worked for McDonald's and got fired for throwing a hamburger at someone through a drive-thru window. The manager did rehire me because he felt sorry for me. I basically cried my way back into the job because I needed the money, and getting fired would have taken my self-esteem even further off track. Ironically, I was the employee of the month three months later after they took me off of cash and put me in the kitchen. I wasn't lazy, but, at that time in my life, I lacked the interpersonal skills and confidence one needed to even be successful at a drive-thru! This is almost laughable now, but every time I remember those times, I am reminded not to make snap judgments about people.

My father always told me to get wide and diverse job experiences when I was young to help figure out what I might like and not like doing for a living. This was at a time in my life when it didn't really matter all that much, so I switched jobs frequently.

I worked drywall and insulation with my brother-in-law on nights and weekends. My entry into automotive started when I ran a lube, oil, and filter pit when I was sixteen, changing oil at Canadian Tire. I was a lot boy at Forest City

Chrysler, worked briefly at the service desk, and I did all sorts of things for the service and sales departments. I also worked on the factory line at Labatt's for a summer job.

I stocked shelves at the Miracle Food Mart Grocery store, and I started a student landscaping business with a friend called D&D Student Lawn Maintenance, which I managed to keep going for seven years (we were nominated by the Royal Bank for the best student business of the year.) I also ran a student paint crew with a company called Paint Brushers. I even had a patent on a novelty item called the "Sneeky Cheeky – the Ultimate Fart Machine." Unfortunately, this genius invention fell by the wayside when I found out that the manufacturing cost was $2, and I couldn't sell it for more than $1.

The point here is that I could also list exactly what I learned about myself; how each and every job led me to my next, and how much I've grown along the way and continue to grow. I've had lots of other jobs working for car dealerships and automotive finance companies, and I have held lots of different positions within those companies—from credit, collections, repossessions to outside and inside sales, closer, management, and training. The one common denominator that I've learned in life professionally is that if you don't evolve, you will dissolve regardless of what you're doing. In addition to companies, this holds true for countries as well.

Along the same timeline, but on a more personal note, right after my fiancé and I decided to get married at only 22, she developed cancer—Hodgkin's disease. She is solely responsible for rebuilding so much of my lost confidence. She was also paying for university through athletic and academic grants while working one or two jobs. It was hard news for us to get at 22. We both temporarily removed ourselves from school so she could start treatments, to then return later that year and complete our degrees.

Shortly after, my best friend Stephen Gomez died very suddenly from a brain aneurysm on Friday the 13th. He was at my wedding party just three months before, and none of my family even came to his funeral or burial. That's how distant I was from my family at that time.

Meanwhile, my landscaping business was terminated because my second business partner Terry Thornhill died from lung cancer.

As a final blow, and at about the same time, a horrendous thing happened in my family. I will not detail it here, but it completely destroyed most relationships on both sides. And all of these events happened within about a three-year time span.

The magnitude of all of this took its toll on my nervous system, my relationships, and my emotional state. I was already an introvert with a struggling attitude going into them, so you can only imagine what all that did to me. It was not a pleasant or easy time for me. My wife calls it my "Dark Time".

Then, one day, while I was working for General Motors, I saw a job opening for a national trainer posted in the office. People often ask me, "How did you get into this? How did you start this?" I didn't even know what a trainer was when I first applied for the job.

What I did know was that the position required five to six days a week of travel for at least a year. When you're as unhappy as I was with my life at that time, travel on someone else's dime means escape.

In the midst of all this, I somehow convinced the hiring managers in Toronto & Detroit that I could become a motivating sales trainer—in spite of the "good advice" that I was totally incapable of this from the cruel, arrogant and incompetent managers I was working for.

Instead of encouraging me to go for it, they called me names and told me I should be thankful to even have the job I had. They told me, "Once you go and try to be a trainer, and it doesn't work out, this job won't be waiting for you when you come back for it. Stay where you are Marino."

That exit interview, where they tried to demean and bully me into not advancing myself, gave me some major motivation. To say I disliked them would be a vast understatement. My motivation at that point was to spite them and show them how little they really knew me. I wanted to prove to them that they had made a mistake in calling me those names and telling me I wasn't capable of doing it. Early on, this really was the fuel that motivated me to succeed. Running away from personal problems and fueled by spite, I had the energy and reasons to really go for it.

The next thing I knew, my daughter was born, and I had to go on the road to save myself. Off I went to Birmingham, Alabama at Key Royal Automotive, spending a few weeks with some very strong salespeople and sales trainers. I met two great guys, Skippy and Sal, and I started to pay attention to some of the books they told me to read.

I began sipping the "Kool-Aid" (accepting the data, unquestionably, without critical examination). Then I started to drink the Kool-Aid hard for a long time. The information they taught me during that time was a springboard into the world of professional sales. It was a "gateway drug" into all the wonderful things I began to study, experience, and master, helping myself and countless others along the way.

By studying them, I started to see how I could become a

good facilitator and an effective salesperson as well as how to improve my sales and myself.

Looking back, I was issued a "White Belt" in sales and sales training back in Birmingham from those masters, and I have been exposing myself to other disciplines and keep training hard in the attempt to gain "Master" status, which always seems to be a moving target. Just as you think you are at the top of your game, you come across something else you want to improve on, or the market changes, and you have to reinvent yourself.

I am always my first guinea pig. Before I teach anyone anything, I have to use it and prove it true and useful for myself. That way I can say with confidence if something works or not, and the problems you might encounter when you try it.

Being my first guinea pig in terms of improving my own life and attitude was one of the best decisions I've ever made in my career because I walked the talk all along the way. Once I really knew what worked and what didn't, I then became addicted to helping other people in the same way that those guys in Birmingham had helped me, and that is still what drives me to this day.

During a period of four years, with the support and friendship of Max S. and Carlo P., this disaster was starting to think he could become a master.

Life and Curve Balls

Life will always throw you curve balls. As I said, my daughter tore her Achilles tendon right in front of me at a home game on her birthday weekend. That was the end of her school soccer career, and she is now regrouping and getting her master's. My son, recovering from a brutal concussion, has switched his major and is training to possibly run track instead of play soccer. They are being personally challenged as never before, and it is true that sometimes we have to dig through a whole lot of garbage to find the real gems of wisdom buried beneath.

I can't imagine what would have happened to me and my business if, on September 13th, 2001, I hadn't sat down and written my goals and gratitudes. As a supplier to the car industry, my professional life was again devastated by the complete collapse of the retail automotive sales training industry in 2008-2009.

I had a year in there that was worse than my first year or two when I was just starting off. I suddenly had no customers willing to spend any money on training as many of them were just trying to hang on to their franchises in the midst of an economic collapse. It was a brutal time because all the dealers everywhere stopped training and advertising.

Ironically, it was this advertising dip that prompted St. Clair Broadcasting out of Washington to do a nationally televised special on sales, with me as its host. With that downtime and financial stress, I had to reinvent myself again, so I made a commitment to build a huge online training portal—MarinoTV—started a call center for my clients called TNT BDC For Hire, helped grow my families used car lot, started this book, acquired some income properties and promised to create any other secondary sources of passive income I could. Now that things have turned around economically, and everyone is back on their feet, all of those ventures are finally coming to fruition and paying me back. If I hadn't evolved, I would have dissolved.

I took another hit on a personal level when my father passed away in 2012. This was absolutely devastating to me and my family. My father was my twin, biggest hero, my mentor, and my biggest fan. I'm sure some of you can relate to the pain of losing your best friend and parent at the same time.

I can tell you with complete certainty that in many ways, I am a better person for having those unpleasant times behind me, as I have learned things about myself and this universe that I would have never learned otherwise.

As I sit in a Starbucks writing this final chapter, my mother is living with my very loving and caring sister and is trying to recover from major surgery to correct a near fatal health problem. And yesterday was spent at the cancer clinic with my wife. She was cancer-free for twenty-five years, and it has now returned to her breast. And she is dealing with it as intelligently and bravely as she did at 22.

Why am I telling you all this? Because parts of my life probably look a lot like yours! Sometimes life sucks and there is nothing you can do about it at that time. All we can do is deal with the cards we are dealt and know not all things are within our control. Just try to become a little wiser, more tolerant, and more compassionate and patient along the way.

Duane Brain Tip

Reader, I think we should all be regularly reminded to not cling to impermanent things, not crave things we cannot or should not have, and not let ignorance or lack of knowledge hold back our growth. If we can remove the causes of suffering, we will find more peace and happiness in any situation. Fewer mistakes means more success! Much of this book has been about avoiding the most common mistakes in sales.

Let's all try to enter every day and every situation with the right intentions, right views, take the right actions, use the right speech for that situation, pay attention to our livelihood, use the right effort, stay mindful and concentrate on the task at hand.

Utilization of Your Potential

Imagine a folder or computer drive in front of you that contains every detail of your entire life. Imagine that this folder also contains all the personal and professional potential that you've been given, the choices you have and could have made, a list of all the people and groups that you could have helped, all the money you could have made, all the debt you could have paid off, all the skills you could have acquired and developed, and the full gamut of emotions that you have felt, had the capacity to feel and make others feel. If your life file was in front of you right now, and it had all of that in it, I ask you, on a scale of one to ten, how much of your vast potential are you utilizing?

"Reality is far greater than the objective, measurable physical world."
—*Tom Campbell, NASA Physicist*

With ten being everything, and one being none at all, go to a mirror, look yourself in your right eye, and ask yourself how much of your potential you use. Three? Five? Eight? I doubt any of us would be a ten. If you are a ten, then raise the bar!

The ultimate goal is to really make the maximum use of

your own personal potential. I hope this book helps you to achieve a little more of that in the areas we have reviewed. I hope you found it motivating, inspiring, and educating and a good use of your precious non-renewable time.

In a horse race, the horse that is going to win the race only has to be better by a nose. In fact, a photo finish may literally mean you're only better by a hair. Your competition is not your enemy, nor is it at the dealership down the road, the other brand, or even the other salesperson. Your real competition stares back at you in your bathroom mirror every morning, and he or she is the only thing that you can control.

Taking control of yourself every day begins with asking yourself, "What can I do today to be a nose better than I was yesterday?" Look at your goals and gratitudes while you ask yourself this. Ask it through the day, at home and work. If that question becomes a daily repetitive habit you're going to have an amazing life with all kinds of things that you will accomplish and some will literally amaze you. After a few years of living this way it may seem like nothing short of a miracle to you and those that know you.

In Conclusion

If I haven't met you already, I'm sure I will at some point in time. I humbly thank you for taking the time to read my book.

I hope you check us out in person at a workshop at one of our Academies, in your region or on-site at your company.

Watch hundreds of powerful sales building and profit recovery tips online with Marino TV available 24/7/365.

Allow our BDC for hire to do a TNT Traffic FLOW Event

for you by calling your customers, activating their buying cycle, booking appointments for you, and sending you the leads.

Follow us on social media sites such as Twitter, LinkedIn, Facebook, YouTube, and Pinterest.

Also, join our monthly email newsletter of selling tips on www.DuaneMarino.com and "Tips by Text" by texting the word "Success" to 71441.

Last but not least, you should also thank yourself, from yourself. To put the time, energy and focus to get through a book is praise-worthy. As I said much earlier, very few people will finish a book that they pick up. Most do not make it past the introductory pages. You're obviously exceptional for getting this far.

I'm Duane Marino. My original purpose in the early 1990s was to study material, such as this, to just help myself. But that soon developed into wanting to help others with their success. This now includes *you* specifically! I hope you create a great career for yourself and see more success than you could ever hope for!

I'm your friend in the sales training business!

Bonus Chapter 15

Appointment Lock Down

Making an appointment is not very difficult, but making one that a person will actually show up for requires a bit more skill. Your three measurable metrics when you book appointments are to have more appointments show up, more who call ahead to cancel (a respectful move that usually results in a rebooking), and reduce or eliminate no-shows. Here are suggestions to help you with all three goals simultaneously by increasing the value of yourself and your time, and put a bit of old-fashioned obligation into the call.

Remember to try to create and listen for curiosity, confusion or interest, and, as soon as you sense any of it, lock it down. Check your posture, and smile on the phone!

Here is the list:

- "Are you normally available during the day or evening?" (Embedded presupposition that one of those general times works, which it does for almost everyone. From this area of agreement you can move forward.)
- "Today or tomorrow?"
- "Beginning of the week or towards the end?"
- "___day or ___day?" (E.g. Monday or Tuesday?)
- "Ok, so … (state the month and day.)"

- "I have __:10 or __:50 available, which is better?" (Use odd times such as ___:20 and ___:40, and push their time by 10 minutes.)

- "Do you know where we're located? Can I text or email you a door-to-door Google Maps link?"

- "I'll hold my calls, get the car ready and make sure an appraiser is here."

- "If your schedule changes, please call me, and, if mine does, I'll do the same for you."

- "Could I have your cell number in case you are running late or are caught in traffic?"

- "Sorry, what time did we say?"

- "By the way, if there is anyone else helping with selection, pricing, or paperwork—even kids, clients, or pets—feel free to bring them as we have an open house environment."

- "If you are replacing something, please bring any extra key fobs, bring in the title, insurance and payoff, and have it cleaned out."

- If the appointment is more than six hours away, always reconfirm it!

Confirmation Contact

- Use subtle psychology to increase your value by emphasizing the "S" in the word "appointments". "I'm confirming all of my appointmentS for today, and I wanted to make sure we are still on for 11:10, :20, :40 or :50," and then remind them to bring in any documentation or people they may need, the second set of keys for their trade, etc.

No-Show Follow-Up

- Follow-up no-shows by blaming it on yourself: "I may have missed you when you came in or written down the wrong time."

- Show concern for them: "Did anything happen? Are you ok?"

- Then rebook the appointment: "So, when can we reschedule?"

- And conclude with a friendly, warm statement such as, "Well, it's always nice to know you have a friend in the car business, isn't it?"

- Top salespeople aren't on the phones because they are busy; they are busy because they are on the phones a lot!

Afterword

Duane's up-to-date pictures, biography, accurate calendars and major accomplishments are on his website, www. DuaneMarino.com, in writing on the Internet, so you can check it out on your own. "Everything we cover is factual and verifiable. Everything. We don't use bogus statistics, make false claims or statements during training about our business or ourselves. We and our customers don't tolerate exaggerated B.S. or lies by omission; it gives the profession a bad name." Duane still sells cars regularly and holds a current sales license.

"We have grown every year since 1995, and almost all of our business is repeats and referrals."

Duane speaks and consults over 200 days a year across Canada and the United States, has trained over 35,000 automotive professionals and over 800+ outstanding dealerships. Clients trust Duane for their professional development. His business is helping your business, and both businesses are about people!

Core services include Duane's Toronto NAASSA Academy that focuses on training Sales Managers, Sales People, F&I Specialists, and Service Advisors every month. FLOW Selling for the entire sales team; on-site, in-dealership training; month-long turnarounds; regional seminars and events; audio CD sets, and online training through MarinoTV. His TNT "Make My Month!" BDC For Hire can help you make your month. And bi-monthly TNT's will make this year your best yet!

- Duane is a consultant, trainer and strategist.

- Duane entered the automotive industry in 1983 and has run the lube rack, been a lot porter, sold (and sells cars today), done credit and collections, repossessed cars, been a car loans officer, set up floor plans, was field rep for an automotive finance company, was national sales trainer for an automotive brand and finance arm, managed, F&I, headed a used car lot, and worked as a closer. Please click on "Our Bios" at www.DuaneMarino.com for more details.

- Duane graduated from the University of Western Ontario.

- Duane found his passion in helping others succeed when he began training and consulting in 1992.

- SELLS CARS TODAY: Duane is active in the retail car business today, selling and managing at his family's used car store (founded in 1968) as well as working with customers at his clients' dealerships.

- ONLY CANADIAN TO ADDRESS THE ANNUAL NADA INTERNATIONAL AUTOMOTIVE CONVENTION: the National Automotive Dealers Association hosts an annual convention that brings automotive suppliers, dealers, executives, managers, and visionaries together.

- FATHERED THE CRM BUSINESS: in 1996, Duane fathered the CRM industry for car dealers, developing and distributing the very first CRM automotive piece—RelMark Relationship Marketing Software—

across North America with clients from Las Vegas to Halifax.

- NUMBER ONE SALES PERSON IN THE WORLD: in 2007, Duane was contacted personally by Joe Girard (www.JoeGirard.com—the world's #1 retail car salesperson) to do a talk with him in the atrium of the Automotive Hall of Fame in Detroit, Michigan where Joe was inaugurated.

- PERFORMANCE GUARANTEE: in 2010, Duane created the first "You Don't Pay Unless They Perform and Stay" training, performance, and invoicing policy, which allows a dealership to train any of their sales-people and enjoy a no-risk performance guarantee window before being invoiced for the training.

- TRADEMARKED "FLOW SELLING": in 2011, Duane began the roll out of a totally modern and fully trademarked sales solution "FLOW Selling", which is changing the "Road to a Sale"; and "The Basics" for salespeople; and replacing both "Step" and "Menu" selling in the F&I department while getting tremen-dous results everywhere.

- LARGEST AND MOST CURRENT ONLINE TRAINING: in 2013, Duane developed from the ground up an entirely new online learning platform, MarinoTV, with over 2000 web-streamed, modern training chapters for every department of the dealer-ship—no rebadged 1990's stuff or hyped up general sales information.

- CLEVELAND ACADEMY OPENS TO MIRROR TORONTO SERVICES: launched NAASSA in Cleveland, Ohio offering our full service workshops, in-dealership and online MarinoTV virtual training.

- CREATOR OF "TNT" TRAFFIC EVENTS: these repeatable phone campaigns using our BDC For Hire professional phone staff will fill your pipeline with fresh, interested buyers, and will never mess up your customer base.

- NATIONAL TV APPEARANCES: Duane is the only Canadian trainer to have ever appeared on National American Television (ABC, NBC, CBC, FOX).

- Duane never accepts, "pay-unders" or thank you bonuses to associations, companies or their representatives and stays completely independent, so you never have to worry about conflicts of interest or outside influences.

- Duane regularly works with retail phone, showroom, and F&I traffic while training at his clients' dealerships, walking the talk, and showing them how to use his techniques in the real world.

- Duane seeks to be a deep enhancement but not necessarily a replacement to whatever selling systems you currently utilize and has respectfully attended dozens of workshops, has read over 400 books, and has spent tens of thousands of dollars on his own learnings in various topics related to sales, selling, the sciences of achievement, and the arts of fulfillment.

- Duane is a trainer, with an open mind, who believes in attending training of all types and has an extensive education in practical psychology. He is certified in several disciplines related to body language, peak performance psychology, health and wellness, sports psychology, sales language, time management, goal setting, state management, and sales psychology.

• Duane is a member of the International Association of Coaching.

• Duane is a volunteer mentor for the North American Youth Business Foundation.

• Duane is frequently asked to contribute his concepts and ideas to various trade publications and magazines.

• Duane has been at the same permanent training facility in downtown Toronto since 1996, which comfortably accommodates groups of 10 to 200 students.

• The top seminar promoters Bob Mohr (USA) and John Kostakos (Canada) promote Duane across North America.

INDEX

A

Acutely aware 43
Adapt your language 102
Appointment Lockdown 118
Appointment Lock Down 263

B

Become Favorably Memorable 14
Becoming Favorably Memorable 188
Be Enjoyable and Interesting 14
Before Google 77, 82, 93, 95, 112, 188
Best Time to Sell 63, 104, 231
Blaming everybody else 43, 49
Blind spot 60, 61
Blueprint of sound Principles 17
Body Language 11, 12, 55, 65, 66, 95, 104, 139, 165, 169, 219, 220,
    221, 222, 224, 225, 226, 227, 229, 230, 240, 241
  Blushing and flushing 228, 229
  Center of gravity changes 227
  Directional body orientation 228
  Eye movements 226, 227
  Microexpressions 225, 226
  Proximity 140
Body Language Signals 221
  Happy Trance 223
  Sudden Negative Realization 223
  Sudden Positive Realization 222
Body language workshops 65
Bonding properties of humor 155
Build Relationships by Being Natural 13
Business vs. "Busyness" 25
Busyness 26

Buyer's psychology 84

C

Calibration: assessing communication 224
Change your self-talk 240
Closing ratio 22, 74, 126, 180
Comfort Zones 40, 42, 47
Compartmentalize your life 210, 234
Consistency of a law or principle 10
Create a schtick 191
Creatures of Habit 20
Critical Mass Numbers 185
Cross refer customers 196
Crucial non-removable traits
Customer Relation Management 15
Customer shoulds or shouldn'ts 94

D

Desired income 42
Dominant Needs Analysis 120
Don't step on anybody's toes 36

E

Effective Use of Time 6, 207
Eliminating your unproductive time 212
Email traffic 83
Emotional Comfort Zone 47, 48
Emotional Quotient (EQ) 44
Entrainment 146, 228
Evolve or Dissolve 252
Exact specifications 80
Experience without growth 52
Eye on Communication 165

F

Fear of rejection 23
Fear of the phones 119
Finance & Insurance Sales 54

Financial Comfort Zone 42, 46
Finishing statement 124
Five Most Important Sales Steps 115
  Confirmed Appointments 115
  Follow-up 133
  Great Demonstration 124
  Proper Checking-in of Trade 119
  Round Number Ranges 129
Five Personality Types 147
  Amiable Communicators 147
  Analytical Decision Makers 149
  Chameleon 150
  Drivers 150
  Expressive Communicators 148
Five P's 5, 9
FLIP Method 239
FLOW Selling 54, 79, 91, 111, 115, 129, 133, 261
Follow-up
  Birthdays 196
  Easy to contact 194
  Remove the Nightmares 198
  Service Valet 193
  Smartphone as a CRM tool 199, 200, 201, 202, 203
    Sharing a common carrier 205

G

Getting a buyer's FORM 141
  F is for Family 141
  M is for Money 144
  O is for Occupation 143
  R is for Recreation 143
Goals and gratitudes 243
  Beliefs control energy 245
    Create a rule set and evidence 247
Google reference and tag names 204
Growth and Improvement Prerequisites 60
  Habituate 64
  Recognize 60
  Reorganize 62

H

Habitual comfort zones 57
Handshake Language 164
Head, heart and gut 18, 19, 71, 189

I

Identify what works and what doesn't 60
Incorrect information 29
Intention-based selling 109
Internet
  Value-building setup tool 83
Introverts & Extroverts 151
Inventory discrepancies 97

K

Know What's in Your Inventory 96

L

Language Patterns 158
Law of 250
Law of 2500
Lead with your heart 110
Learning by Experience 51
Learning by Modeling 55
Learning by Trial and Error 51, 55, 57
Level One Selling 178, 179, 186
Level Three Selling 184, 186
Level Two Selling 181, 186
Listening 139, 140
Listening is the by-product of respect 220
Long-Term Perspective 25

M

Mental Rehearsal 62
Mirroring People 146, 149, 155, 220, 242
Motivational rituals
  Before leaving for work 209

N

Negative attitudes 43
Negative issues 19
Non-severable association 184
Nutrition is important 243

O

Openness Quotient (OQ) 44
Overt rapport 163

P

Pareto Principle 177
Patterns 9, 17, 21, 158
Perception is reality. 161
Performance Psychology 5, 39
Personal Set Points 40
Phone Chump vs. Phone Champ 118
Planned Sales Responses
  Accompanied Test Drive 135
  Immediate "Be Back" Follow-Up 137
  Setting an Appointment 134
  Talking Price Ranges Early 136
  Trade-in 134
Potential Sale
Powerful authentic relationships 189
Power of Focus 208, 231
Power Profiling 166
Practices are strategies 11
Probability 9, 17, 22
Professional and Consistent Social Media 192
Professional sales career 31
Psychology 5, 4, 9, 16, 17, 19, 39
Psychology of the Buyer 19
Public vs. Private Information 173, 174

R

Reading via a script 13
Result goals vs. Activity goals 48

Round number ranges 129

S

Sales Glue 155, 158
Sales Language 102, 167
  Old vs. New
Salesperson vs. Someone in Sales 59
Sales Psychology 4
Sales puzzle. 113
Scotoma 60
Self-sabotage 45
Self-talk 240, 241, 246
Sell like an angel 4
Sensory acuity: assessing sales cycle 224
Set Points 42, 47
Shortcut to success 52, 68
Six crucial skills 6
Six Sales Powers 1, 3, 5, 6, 99, 100, 105, 248
  Body Language 104
  Building Relationships 13, 103, 109, 139
  Communication and Sales Language. 102
  Customer Service 5, 101, 109
  Making Effective Use of Time 103
  State of Mind and Focus 104
Skin in the game
Soft sales statistics 69
Specific product information 89
Statistics vs. Trends 5, 69
Stay off price 77, 82
Successful people walk with 242
Surface appearance of wealth 144
Survey Business Prospecting 183

T

Tenacity formula 234
Text management during the sale 202
Threee things that effect success 251
Three ways to get out of a job 33
Time Comfort Zone 46

Time management 86, 103, 104
Time-sensitive 47
Time trap audits 208
Touching the emotional 16
Trade vs. a Profession 30
Trend is your friend 70, 71
Tribal Laws 152
Two Common Deadly Traits 64

U

Understanding their motivations 145
Using Colorful Language 154
Utilization of Your Potential 260

V

Verbal language 11
Victim vs. Victor 212
Victim vs. Victor
 213, 214
Video testimonials 203
Vitamin L deficiency 30, 105, 106, 110, 134, 138

W

Walk-in traffic 83, 182, 212
Walk-in Traffic 15
What's wrong with the car? 93, 120
Winning More Losing Less 232
word-of-mouth promotion 2

Y

Your online presence

Next time you're having a bad day, think of this. Duane holds it in his hand often, and it has inspired him since he was a small boy...

"My father spent his child hood running from bombs. At 14 he ran away, alone, as a war refugee. At 17, he found his way to Canada by himself, wearing this tag around his neck. Marked "No Baggage", "To Be Fed" and notched with his meal stamps. Put on the boat he was destined to be a "Labourer" but made himself a certified machinist in a new language before he was 25, and he never went past grade 3 back home. He was a displaced war refugee, having lost his home, his city Pola, several friends and his brother. With nothing to lose he came here and built a life to be proud of. My mentor, my best friend and my biggest fan. Love you Pops. Respected you always. Miss you everyday. Can't wait till next time around...they say 3 is the charm. ;) " Duane Marino

1

Achieve Profit Through Process

CPSIA information can be obtained at www.ICGtesting.com
Printed in the USA
LVOW05s0819160615

442644LV00017B/77/P